GREAT FLOWERING
LANDSCAPE TREES

GREAT FLOWERING
LANDSCAPE TREES

VINCENT A. SIMEONE

{ Photography by Bruce Curtis, Foreword by Irene Virag, Preface by Fred Soviero }

 Ball Publishing | Batavia, Illinois

Ball Publishing
P.O. Box 9
335 N. River Street
Batavia, IL 60510
www.ballpublishing.com

ISBN 978-1-883052-53-9

Library of Congress Cataloging-in-Publication Data

Simeone, Vincent A.
  Great flowering landscape trees / Vincent A. Simeone ; photographs by
Bruce Curtis.
      p. cm.
  Includes bibliographical references and indexes.
  ISBN 978-1-883052-53-9 (hardcover : alk. paper)
  1. Flowering trees--Varieties--United States. 2. Flowering trees--United
States--Nomenclature. 3. Landscape gardening--United States. I. Title.

  SB435.5.S56 2007
  635.9'7713--dc22
                          2006103160

Printed in Singapore by Imago.
9 8 7 6 5 4 3 2 1 07 08 09 10 11 12 13

Dedication

This book is dedicated to my friends and mentors: Allan and Susan Armitage, David and Eileen Barnett, Gary and Jean Brown, Michael and Bonnie Dirr, Linda and Steve Finley, Gordon and Thelma Jones, John and Connie Norbeck, Sal and Peggy Pezzino, Fred and Ronnie Soviero, Peter and Dori Tilles, Owen and Bernadette Smith, James and Liz Watson, Harvey Aronson, Irene Virag, and David Catalano. I am truly a better person for having been touched by these great people. Life is only as good as the people around you!

6/5/09

Happy Gardening!

Sincerely,

Vincent Simeone

v

Crabapples flowering in the landscape

I think that I shall never see

A poem lovely as a tree.

A tree whose hungry mouth is prest

Against the sweet earth's flowing breast;

A tree that looks at God all day,

And lifts her leafy arms to pray;

A tree that may in summer wear

A nest of robins in her hair;

Upon whose bosom snow has lain;

Who intimately lives with rain.

Poems are made by fools like me,

But only God can make a tree.

—*Joyce Kilmer, "Trees," 1914*

Table of Contents

Flowering cherry and cottage

"The cultivation of trees
is the cultivation of
the good, the beautiful,
and the ennobling in man."

—*J. Sterling Morton,*
1832–1902,
founder of Arbor Day

Acknowledgments

A special thank you to the Bridgehampton Community House, Bridgehampton, New York; C. W. Post Community Arboretum, Brookville, New York; Hofstra Arboretum, Hempstead, New York; New York Botanical Garden, Bronx, New York; and Planting Fields Arboretum State Historic Park, Oyster Bay, New York, which allowed us to photograph a wide variety of flowering trees. Also, I would like to extend my sincere gratitude to the collaborators on this book: Patrick Cullina, Bruce Curtis, Donna Moramarco, Gloria Simeone, Fred Soviero, and Irene Virag. Thanks also go out to Richard Gibney of the Gibney Design Group, Wading River, New York, for the use of his tree planting illustrations.

Foreword

Flowering dogwood trees brought poetry to the springs of my childhood. There were none growing in the yard of my Bridgeport, Connecticut, home, but each year a festival celebrating dogwoods bloomed in a neighboring community. I always thought how nice it would be to have one of my own. So, when I grew up and moved into my own house across the sound on the North Shore of Long Island, I was charmed by the sight of two dogwoods on my property.

The white blossoms of my *Cornus florida* touch past and present each year as the earth warms. I became a gardener and started branching out. A kousa dogwood took root at the edge of my lawn, and a star magnolia received a place of honor in a new bed outside the study window. A venerable Japanese cherry tree canopies the patio, and each spring its falling blossoms form a pink carpet over brick and bluestone. And by the gate leading to the backyard, a crape myrtle heralds autumn.

When I lost a weeping cherry tree last year, I cried. I missed its delicate grace and, most of all, its pale pink blossoms. I worry that some of us get so caught up in nurturing annuals and perennials that sometimes we don't see the trees for the flowers. But there are so many trees whose blooms enhance our lives as well as our landscapes.

My own affection for flowering trees blossomed when I met my friend Vincent Simeone. I will always treasure his patience with a fledgling garden writer and his generosity with his time and expertise. On our first walk through Planting Fields Arboretum, where he is now the director, I thought, *Now, here's a man who truly loves trees.* Vinnie is a tree-hugger, and I mean that literally. He really does hug trees, and I understand why. I hugged my weeping cherry when it was dying.

Vinnie's knowledge and enthusiasm flower throughout this book. He talks for the trees. For old favorites and new cultivars. For bottlebrush buckeyes and Carolina silverbells and goldenrain trees and stewartias. For saucer magnolias and weeping mulberries and flowering quinces and September sumac—and dozens more. He tells us how to plant them, prune them, care for them, treasure them. You'll find it hard to read this book without turning into a tree-hugger yourself.

Irene Virag
Garden columnist

Preface

It is my distinct privilege to have been asked to write the preface to this book. Vincent Simeone writes with knowledge of his subject and a passion that comes through between the lines.

What is your favorite tree? This is a question I have been asked on numerous occasions, and each time I have to stop and think. Can you pick one favorite when you see the beauty and possibilities in each and every tree you plant? Years ago, when I was studying horticulture and had to write a thesis on any tree of my choosing, I picked *Fagus sylvatica*, the European beech. I suppose it was because I was captivated with ones I had seen so far in my short career. The smooth, gray bark, appearing as elephants standing in the forest. The tremendous size of those that reached for my attention and the presence they held in the landscape. These were trees worth delving into.

I wanted my bibliography to be long and extensive, probably so I could impress my teacher, but in doing so, my passion for trees began. Ten years later my wife, Ronnie, who was pregnant in her last trimester, and I were out walking and came upon a most beautiful tree, with the most delicate and fragrant summer flowers. The tree we were admiring was a linden, and we decided to name our third child, if she was a girl, after this wonderful gem. We dared not name her Tilia. Lindyn was born on June 26, 1986. I don't believe you can pick a favorite tree, or a favorite child for that matter, unless you have but one. They are all my favorites.

On the following pages you will explore choices of trees that will grace any landscape—some quite familiar, others you never knew existed. *Albizia julibrissin* 'Summer Chocolate', the mimosa or hardy silk tree, which has leaves so fragile with the hue of chocolate you could almost eat them. And then there is the downy serviceberry, *Amelanchier arborea*, a favorite native tree with early spring blooms of silky white and deep purple fruits whose taste rival the best of blueberries. On guided tours the author has been known to strip these trees clean of fruit like a swarm of locusts, so get there soon after they ripen, or the birds and Vinnie will surely beat you to the table.

In addition to offering valuable information on the aesthetic value, cultural requirements, and landscape functions of trees, *Great Flowering Landscape Trees* offers a section on proper planting, pruning, and general maintenance practices. The advice here is gathered from Vinnie's experience at Planting Fields Arboretum as well as through his extensive education and network of plant professionals. The success of our landscapes is based on scientific principles such as these and should be carefully considered. The attention we pay to planting and aftercare cannot be overstated. We know that "mighty oaks from tiny acorns grow." We can guarantee that fact by being responsible stewards of our gardens.

Choose wisely and enjoy!

Fred Soviero
Hofstra University Arboretum

About This Book

What would the landscape be without flowering trees? Undoubtedly rather mundane. Flowering trees provide unique structure, texture, and color in the landscape all year, but especially in the spring and summer seasons. Now more then ever gardeners crave choice species and varieties of trees to brighten up their landscape.

Great Flowering Landscape Trees provides garden lovers with a useful reference for choice flowering trees suitable for a wide variety of landscape uses. Within each plant description, important information on select plant species including ornamental value, landscape value, care, and culture are offered in this book.

From beautiful flowers to radiant fall color to luscious ornamental fruit, flowering trees dazzle us with many ornamental qualities. *Great Flowering Landscape Trees* is a hands-on, practical guide to some old favorites as well as some new and exciting introductions.

Read on and enjoy!

A Brief Introduction to Flowering Trees

Flowering trees are a very important component of the overall garden scheme. A landscape graced with beautiful flowering trees can be magical during the spring and summer months. The spectacular succession of bloom from magnolias, dogwoods, cherries, and crabapples is like a well-choreographed fireworks display.

As a child I would anticipate with great enthusiasm the unfurling of dogwood flowers, cherry blossoms, and a large, old-fashioned crabapple that grew outside my bedroom window. My first horticulture job—at Moffit Garden Center, a local retail nursery—further heightened my curiosity in woody plants, as did observing local residents busily planting their newfound trees throughout the neighborhood. It was then that I realized that flowering trees were an integral part of the environment in which we live. They are like faithful old friends, and flowering trees continue to amaze me with their unrivaled beauty, landscape function, and versatility.

The goal of this book is to celebrate the beauty, importance, and function of some well-known flowering tree species and also to reveal some lesser-known species that are worthy of inclusion in the garden. Although the main focus is on the flowers themselves, it is also my goal to extol other ornamental virtues that flowering trees offer, such as foliage texture, fall color, fruit, and bark interest. Undoubtedly, the best flowering tree is one that provides rich, colorful floral displays in spring but also shines in other seasons of the year. There are in fact many trees offered in this book that present three and four seasons of interest. Over the past two decades many beautiful new varieties of flowering trees have been developed for the home garden. This new research has yielded improved flower color and size, better foliage color and pest resistance, and greater durability in the landscape. Throughout this book many new and improved varieties of well-known species are mentioned in the hope that the truly passionate gardener will try them in his or her own garden.

Although I began to appreciate trees when I was very young, my true affection for flowering trees and their new, exciting varieties strongly developed as a student at Farmingdale State University and the University of Georgia. There I was amazed at all the new introductions and the efforts by researchers and the nursery industry to select and introduce the next great plant variety. Of course, as a student of Michael Dirr and Allan Armitage at UGA, two great horticulturists, it was not too long before I was mastering the art of searching for the latest, greatest varieties of garden favorites.

Magnolia and cherry blooming in unison

I have also been fortunate to employ this passion as curator of plant collections at Planting Fields Arboretum State Historic Park in Oyster Bay, New York. There I truly began to search out and introduce the newest and brightest that the horticulture industry has to offer. Today these trees provide an aesthetically pleasing and educational experience enjoyed by the arboretum's visiting public.

Gardening is an ever-changing, challenging, and exciting voyage that has endless possibilities. Flowering trees are one of many valuable components of that experience. Through all of the continuous changes that happen in the garden, one thing is certain: There is a whole new world just waiting to be discovered. Enjoy the journey!

USING PLANT NAMES

Both scientific plant names and common names are an important part of everyday gardening life. Scientific names are written in Latin, the universal language in the horticultural world. Scientific names are basically comprised of a genus name, also referred to as generic term, and a specific epithet. Such *binomial nomenclature* is important to understand, especially when researching or purchasing plants from a local nursery or garden center.

A *genus* is a group of closely related plants comprising one or more species. The *specific epithet* identifies the specific member of the genus. The two names together precisely identify a particular species. For example, the scientific name for Oriental flowering cherry is *Prunus* (genus) *serrulata* (specific epithet).

When discussing multiple species of the same genus, it is common to use only the initial of the genus name. Here's a passage from this book's *Prunus* section: "Many species and varieties of *Prunus* can be used in the residential landscape. Three of the most commonly available are Oriental cherry (*P. serrulata*), weeping Higan cherry (*P. subhirtella* 'Pendula'), and Yoshino cherry (*P.* x *yedoensis*)."

In addition to a scientific name, every plant is typically assigned a *common name*, which often describes a notable physical or other unique characteristic of the plant. For example, the saucer magnolia (*Magnolia* x *soulangiana*) offers large, goblet-sized blooms in spring, each of which, as it unfurls, looks like a cup and saucer. (The "x" in the scientific name means it's a hybrid, or a cross between two species.)

Common names tend to create confusion, though. They can vary between regions, so a given plant may have multiple common names. For instance, *Amelanchier canadensis* is referred to as shadblow, serviceberry, and Juneberry. Conversely, a given common name may refer to several unrelated plants. Take "burning bush": it refers to a species within the genus *Euonymus* (also known as spindle tree, winged euonymus, and wahoo), the shrub *Bassia scoparia* (also firebush, fireball, Mexican fireweed, summer cypress, and belvedere), rambling tropical shrubs of the genus *Combretum* (flame creeper, flame keeper, fire vine), or the perennial herb *Dictamnus albus* (gas plant, dittany, fraxinella). As you can see, the one scientific name is more reliable for finding or identifying a plant. It is important for even the casual gardener to learn both scientific and common names.

Some plant names include other terms that are helpful to understand. A *cultivar*, also referred to as a *cultivated variety* or *garden variety*, is cultivated or selected for certain special garden qualities that are distinct from the basic species. Cultivated varieties or garden varieties typically originate in a garden rather than in the wild and have very specific ornamental characteristics and landscape functions that are valuable in the cultivated garden. Cultivar names are capitalized and are usually surrounded by single quotation marks, or you may find the single quotes replaced by the abbreviation *cv.* (for *cultivated variety*). For example, the scientific name for pink kousa dogwood can be written as *Cornus kousa* 'Satomi' or *Cornus kousa* cv. Satomi.

Although the term *variety* in this book commonly designates a garden variety, the true scientific term refers to a naturally occurring variation within a species. Scientific names are written in lowercase letters and without single quotations, following the abbreviation *var.* For example, *Cornus florida* var. *rubra* is the scientific name for pink flowering dogwood, a naturally occurring variety with deep pink flowers rather than the pure white flowers of the straight species (*C. florida*).

Public gardens provide an important service as educational facilities in promoting the vital roles plants play in the environment we live in. These horticultural institutions give interested gardeners the opportunity to learn about a variety of plants that are suitable for the home landscape. One of the most important elements of a good public garden is its displaying of readable, coherent plant labels, with both common and scientific names.

HARDINESS ZONE MAP

The USDA Plant Hardiness Zone Map illustrates the average minimum temperatures of the United States. The map is separated into eleven zones, with 1 representing the coldest zone, 11 the warmest. Although several environmental factors—such as heat, humidity, and rainfall—have an impact on plant adaptability, cold hardiness is one of the most important. It is important to identify the zone where you live to ensure the winter survival of the plants you select. Plants that are tender or marginally hardy in a given hardiness zone may perform poorly or die. The hardiness zone range for each plant species or variety in this book is listed within the text of each plant description.

To learn your hardiness zone, identify the area where you live on the map. There is a zone number assigned to that region. For example, the hardiness zone for Chicago is Zone 5, which has average minimum temperatures of −20 to −10° F. For exact temperature ranges within a given hardiness zone, read the zone key located below the map.

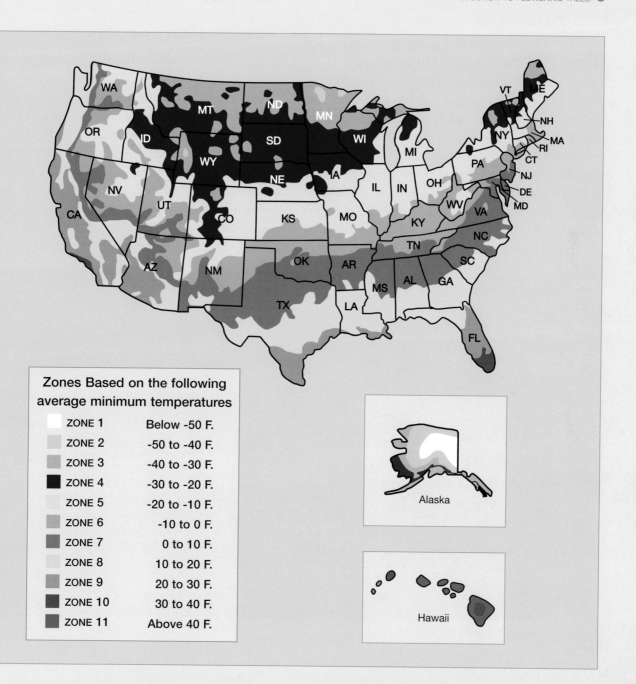

Zones Based on the following average minimum temperatures

	ZONE 1	Below -50 F.
	ZONE 2	-50 to -40 F.
	ZONE 3	-40 to -30 F.
	ZONE 4	-30 to -20 F.
	ZONE 5	-20 to -10 F.
	ZONE 6	-10 to 0 F.
	ZONE 7	0 to 10 F.
	ZONE 8	10 to 20 F.
	ZONE 9	20 to 30 F.
	ZONE 10	30 to 40 F.
	ZONE 11	Above 40 F.

Alaska

Hawaii

NATIVES VERSUS EXOTIC SPECIES

Recent debate has raised questions about the value of native species in the garden and the challenges that invasive exotic species present to our environment. The purpose of this book is to acknowledge the wonderful attributes of exceptional flowering trees that can add beauty and function to the home landscape. It is not intended to alienate you from or exclude any group of plants. This book gives equal attention to worthwhile native trees and excellent exotics as valuable assets to American gardens. It is important to have a diverse landscape with a strong balance of natives and exotic species.

The perception that all exotic species are invasive is a false one. The key to a successful garden and healthy environment is to discourage the infiltration of invasive exotic species whenever possible and to encourage superior natives and noninvasive exotics. If we were to follow the notion that the use of all exotic species should be curtailed, we would never get to experience the wonderful assets of *Stewartia*, *Malus*, magnolia, and so many other garden treasures.

© Bruce Curtis

Flowering dogwood in the landscape

Deciduous Flowering Trees A–Z

© Vincent A. Simeone

Chestnuts flowering in the landscape

© Bruce Curtis

Red chestnut flowers

{ *Aesculus* spp.
Chestnuts and buckeyes
Aesculus x *carnea* (red chestnut)

The red chestnut is a hybrid flowering tree that offers large, cone-shaped flower clusters that stand straight up on the end of each branch in the spring. The deep rosy pink flowers look like candles as they unfurl on the tree. The foliage is a rich, glossy green, with five distinct leaflets that form a palm- or fan-shaped leaf. This medium-size tree can reach 30 to 40 ft. tall, with an equal spread. The growth habit is pyramidal during youth, becoming dense and rounded with age.

Red chestnut prefers moist, well-drained soil, and full sun or partial shade. It benefits from soil that is rich in organic matter. Like one of its parents, the common horse chestnut (*Aesculus hippocastanum*), red chestnut is susceptible to a leaf blotch that causes brown spots on the leaves. Generally, this disease affects the aesthetics of the tree and does not cause serious injury.

Red chestnut is most effectively used as a single specimen in a lawn area or in a small grouping. It is ideal as a lawn tree in the front yard of a home. It is quite popular in Europe, where it is used in parks, public gardens, and other large sites. Red chestnut is hardy from Zones 4–7 and doesn't particularly like hot, dry climates.

NOTABLE VARIETIES

'Briottii'. This variety offers larger and darker red flowers with a yellow throat.

'O'Neill Red'. Striking 10–12 in. flowers and lustrous, glossy green foliage make this a very desirable variety.

'Fort McNair'. This flowering tree, selected at Ft. McNair in Washington, D.C., offers dark pink flowers and deep green, disease-resistant foliage that tends to be more resistant to leaf blotch than other red chestnut varieties.

Aesculus hippocastanum (common horse chestnut)

One of the parent plants of the red chestnut, the common horse chestnut also provides a spectacular floral display in spring. The creamy white flower spikes emerge in midspring as the large, palmately compound leaves are unfolding. After flowering, spiny, green seed capsules form. They open in the fall, dispersing dark brown, smooth, chestnutlike seeds. This fruit is poisonous to humans, and this tree is considered strictly an ornamental.

Although quite beautiful in the spring, it is susceptible to various pests and diseases, including a leaf blotch that causes a scorching of the leaves in midsummer. Because of this and the tree's tendency to grow too large for residential sites, it is not typically recommended for the homeowner. Should you choose to grow this large tree, 'Baumannii' is an improved variety, offering double white flowers for a longer period of time than the species. In addition, this variety does not produce seed. Effective in parks, golf courses, and public gardens.

Aesculus pavia (red buckeye)

This delightful small flowering tree is native to the

© Bruce Curtis
Red buckeye foliage and red flowers

© Bruce Curtis
Red buckeye in the landscape

southeastern United States. It offers glossy, dark green, palmately compound leaves and rather loose, deep red panicles of flowers in spring. The leaves of red buckeye are the finest of any buckeye species. Often as cool weather approaches in the autumn, the leaves will turn a purplish color before falling to the ground. Red buckeye does not grow quite as large as some of the other *Aesculus* species mentioned and is often shrubby in habit, making it ideal for the residential landscape with limited room. The tree reaches an average of 22–25 ft. tall, with a 15–20 ft. spread over time.

Red buckeye is relatively pest free and adapts well to many landscape situations, although it does not like dry, windy sites. For best results plant red buckeye in moist, rich, well-drained soil and full sun or partial shade. It benefits from the cooling light shade provided by larger trees above. Red buckeye performs best in Zones 4–8.

Red buckeye is one of the most beautiful small flowering trees for the home garden. It is very effective as a single-specimen lawn tree or in a small grouping in a larger area of the garden.

Aesculus parviflora (bottlebrush buckeye)

Bottlebrush buckeye is one of the most magnificent flowering trees for summer and fall interest. It typically has a dense, spreading, shrubby habit, but with judicious pruning, it can be trained into a delightful small tree. In early summer 12 in. long, white, bristly flower spikes form and persist for several weeks. The floral display is rather magnificent. The large, palm-shaped, dark green leaves provide a coarse texture during the summer, and they turn bright yellow in autumn. In

© Vincent A. Simeone

Bristly white flowers of bottlebrush buckeye

© Vincent A. Simeone

Foliage and flowers of bottlebrush buckeye

New bronzy foliage of bottlebrush buckeye

© Bruce Curtis

keep plants vigorous. Selective pruning can also be used to limit spreading and keep shrubs in scale.

Bottlebrush buckeye is very effective as a specimen in a lawn area or in a mass planting, either in sun or in a shady part of the garden. It has shown resistance to deer browse. Hardy from Zones 4–8.

Aesculus glabra (Ohio buckeye)

The state tree of the Buckeye State, the Ohio buckeye (*Aesculus glabra*) develops into a large, stately tree with pale yellow flowers and deep green foliage that often changes to orange in the fall. Spiny fruit capsules open to expose smooth, rich brown seeds called buckeyes. These fruits are not edible to humans but are a tasty treat for wildlife.

Aesculus × 'Autumn Splendor' is a hybrid of *A. glabra* selected by the Minnesota Landscape Arboretum for its dark glossy green foliage, turning brilliant red in the fall. Its showy spring flowers are yellow with a red throat.

Albizia julibrissin
Mimosa

Mimosa, or silk tree, is an old favorite that could be found in the frontyards of many residential landscapes several decades ago. Because of its ability to readily propagate itself, one could also find chance seedlings popping up in flowerbeds, along the foundation of the house, or even in the cracks along a sidewalk.

Mimosa is a very delicate tree, with long, dark green, fernlike leaves that are soft to the touch. Soft, puffy pink flowers form in summer and persist for several months. Mimosa in full flower makes quite a spectacular display

addition, during the late summer fruit capsules form, later dispersing smooth, nonedible, chestnutlike fruit.

This reliable garden performer can be interesting during the winter, as well. The slender, gray, upright-growing stems create dense clumps that can become 8–12 ft. tall, with a potentially greater spread. Regular pruning is needed when plants are young to train them into single- or multistemmed flowering trees. This great versatility helps make bottlebrush buckeye one of the most ornamental garden plants available.

Bottlebrush buckeye is a low-maintenance shrub that prefers moist, well-drained, acidic soil with generous amounts of organic matter. It thrives in full sun or partial shade but will tolerate varying soil types and deep shade. Occasional selective pruning to thin out older stems will during the long, hot days of summer. The dense, spreading, vase-shaped habit is also very attractive.

Mimosa tree is very fast-growing, quite adaptable to various soil types, and especially tolerant of heat and drought. Mimosa is hardy from Zones 6–9. However, because of a serious fungal wilt disease, this interesting tree is not as popular as it once was. This disease can damage and eventually kill large, mature specimens.

Several varieties of mimosa are touted for their resistance to the wilt disease and are worthy of planting. 'Charlotte' has light-colored pink flowers, and 'Tryon' offers deeper red flowers. But one of the most unusual and stunning varieties is 'Summer Chocolate', with deep maroon foliage that persists all summer, accented by deep rose–colored flowers. The foliage alone is reason enough to add this plant as an accent to the landscape. The varieties are effective as single specimens in a lawn area or when mixed in combination with other shrubs and herbaceous plants.

Amelanchier spp.
Serviceberry

Serviceberry, also known as shadbush and Juneberry, is a large shrub or small tree that will enhance the landscape all four seasons of the year. This spring-flowering plant offers small, delicate white bouquets of flowers, followed by edible fruit in early summer. The fruits develop from green to red to deep blackish purple when fully ripe and look like small blueberries. The fruit is without question one of the most delectable of any fruit-bearing tree. I have seized many an opportunity to pluck a few tasty fruits from a tree found along a garden walk. Serviceberry fruit can be used to make jams, jellies, and pies if enough can be harvested at one time. Often the birds cleverly beat us to the punch.

These beautiful native American trees offer great seasonal ornamental value and function in the landscape. In the fall serviceberry displays foliage color that changes from yellow to bright orange, red, or maroon,

© Vincent A. Simeone

Lacy, deep maroon foliage of 'Summer Chocolate' mimosa

© Bruce Curtis

Serviceberry flower up close

Serviceberry in the landscape

although sometimes leaf diseases or drought can compromise the leaves during the summer, leaving plants partially or fully defoliated by fall. This situation usually occurs only in years when the tree has to endure severe heat and humidity. Many of the new varieties of serviceberry seem to be resistant to leaf diseases and offer reliable fruiting.

During the winter months, the smooth, silvery gray bark, with noticeable silver streaks or striations, sparkles in the winter landscape. Even the thinnest of branchlets has an attractive silver color. With age, mature specimens develop an upright, dense, and irregular growth pattern, giving them a windswept appearance.

Smooth, silvery gray bark of serviceberry

© Bruce Curtis

Serviceberry can be used in a cultivated garden setting or in a naturalized planting. In flower, from a distance it looks similar to Callery pear and can be used as an appropriate replacement along a building, street, or pathway. Serviceberry is ideal in small groupings near a stream or pond or as a single specimen in a lawn area among other flowering shrubs.

In its native habitat serviceberry thrives in a shady, moist forest setting under the dappled shade of tall trees. Ideally, serviceberry prefers full sun or partial shade and well-drained, moist, acidic soil. Leaf spots, rusts, and other diseases may be a problem under certain environmental conditions, but these durable landscape trees typically tolerate such problems. Sometimes they defoliate prematurely in the late summer or early fall, but they refoliate the following spring. Most species of serviceberry are hardy from Zones 4–8.

Several noteworthy species are available, along with a few select garden varieties. Several of the most common species in the landscape are shadblow serviceberry (*Amelanchier canadensis*), apple serviceberry (*Amelanchier* x *grandiflora*), and Allegheny serviceberry (*Amelanchier laevis*). These species are similar in some respects and quite different in others. All can be grown as either single- or multiple-stemmed small trees but are more often seen as multistemmed.

NOTABLE VARIETIES

'Autumn Brilliance' (*A.* x *grandiflora*). Its beautiful green summer foliage turns shades of brilliant red in the fall, revealing its densely arranged gray stems.

'Ballerina' (*A.* × *grandiflora*). This upright plant has large white flowers in spring and deep green foliage that turns orange-red in fall.

'Cole's Select' (*A.* × *grandiflora*). This interesting variety produces masses of flowers in early spring and sweet, purplish blue fruit in summer. The foliage turns brilliant orange-red in fall.

'Cumulus' (*A. laevis*). This variety of serviceberry has a distinct narrow, upright growth habit, so it can be used in areas with limited space, such as along narrow pathways or in planting areas between streets and sidewalks.

'Princess Diana' (*A.* × *grandiflora*). A variety selected for producing a profusion of showy white flowers in spring and brilliant red fall color, it is also known to be relatively resistant to many leaf diseases.

'Robin Hill' (*A.* × *grandiflora*). It offers pink flower buds that unfold to pale pink or white flowers, and has fall foliage that ranges from yellow to red.

{ *Aralia elata 'Variegata'*
Variegated Japanese angelica tree

This unusual variegated large shrub or small tree offers large, pinnately compound leaves with creamy white coloration along the edges. In summer large, rounded panicles of creamy flowers form at the ends of the branches. Soon after flowering, beautiful small, purple fruit ripen and persist for several weeks. The flower and fruit display is quite effective. The overall growth habit of Japanese angelica tree is layered and umbrellalike. It has a dense, upright habit reaching 10 ft. tall and 6–10 ft. wide. The combination of large, variegated foliage,

Variegated foliage of Japanese angelica tree

© Vincent A. Simeone

flowers, fruit, and growth habit make this an interesting tree from spring through fall.

Japanese angelica tree thrives in moist, well-drained soil and full sun but can easily adapt to varying soil types and partial shade. It is especially tolerant of dry soil. Japanese angelica tree can tolerate drought, heat, and other tough environmental conditions, making it an extremely durable plant. Hardy from Zones 4–9.

Japanese angelica tree can be used as a single specimen, in a grouping, or as an accent plant among herbaceous plants. I have also seen it used very effectively in containers and raised planters. There are several other variegated selections, including 'Aureomarginata', with golden yellow variegated leaves, and 'Silver Umbrella', with a silvery white variegated leaf.

{ *Asimina triloba*
Pawpaw tree

This native American species offers unusual but beautiful flowers in spring, followed by edible fruit in the summer months. The small, bell-shaped, deep purplish brown flowers dangle from each stem. Flowers persist for several weeks before fading. The flowers are followed by elongated, greenish yellow fruit, which ripen to deep brownish black. The fruit has a delightful sweet taste similar to a banana. During the summer months large, glossy green leaves develop and in the fall they turn bright yellow.

Pawpaw prefers rich, organic, well-drained soil and full sun or partial shade. In a cultivated garden setting pawpaw will grow 15–20 ft. tall, but it can get larger in ideal conditions. Hardy from Zones 5–8.

© Vincent A. Simeone

Deep purple flowers of pawpaw

Pawpaw can be used as a single-specimen tree or in groupings. It is also effective as a woodland tree in a partially shaded area of the garden. Although pawpaw is a fairly uncommon tree, its aesthetic qualities and edible fruit make it a valuable addition to the garden. It will undoubtedly stand out among the more traditional flowering trees, such as dogwood, magnolia, and ornamental cherry.

{ *Camellia* spp.
Camellia

Although camellias are considered shrubs in most cultivated gardens, they can grow quite large in mild climates and be trained as small flowering trees, especially in gardens in the southern United States and on the West Coast. As camellias mature, the lower branches can be removed to expose the beautiful smooth, grayish tan bark. Because of their ornamental qualities, adaptability, and function, they are worthy of inclusion in the garden.

Camellia has an extensive, rich garden history and has long been admired as one of the most exotic and romantic of flowering evergreens. During the eighteenth century, camellias were imported to Europe and America from Japan and China, where they grow in the higher elevations of the mountains. For many years they were considered to be tender in cooler climates and were only used in greenhouse collections. But in several parts of the United States, such as the Southeast and the West Coast, camellias grow outdoors.

There are two main species valued as garden ornamentals in America, Japanese camellia (*Camellia japonica*) and Sasanqua camellia (*C. sasanqua*). These ornamental camellias are close relatives of the tea plant (*C. sinensis*), a major economic crop that is used in manufacturing tea. Camellia flowers are incredibly diverse, with many different flower colors and types to choose from. Flower colors range from white to pink to red, and the same flower can even display two colors. Camellia flower types can also vary from single to semidouble or double and can mimic the appearance of such other flowers as peonies and anemones. Equally striking is camellia foliage, which is a handsome dark glossy green.

Camellias have specific cultural needs similar to those of rhododendrons. They thrive in moist, well-drained, acidic soil with high organic content. Camellias prefer light shade, and mulch will also help protect their shallow root systems. Although camellias thrive in moist, cool environments, they are remarkably tolerant of hot, humid conditions, provided they are watered properly. Several pests, including scale and spider mites, can damage camellias. If a pest problem occurs, take a sample to your local agricultural extension service for evaluation and treatment suggestions.

Pruning to shape the plants or to maintain their dense habit can be done after flowering. If severe pruning is needed, wait until late winter or early spring, when the shrubs are still dormant. In a greenhouse or warmer climate, gardeners may have to wait

© Bruce Curtis

Showy flowers and smooth, dark green foliage of camellia

until later in the spring for it to be safe to prune. Severe pruning will reduce flowering the first year but stimulate the plant to produce a healthy crop of flowers the next few years. In general, regular severe pruning should be avoided. Camellias can reach 8–12 ft. in height and 6–10 ft. wide but can be kept smaller with judicious pruning.

Camellias are excellent large flowering shrubs or small trees that add structure and beauty to the home landscape. The long-lasting flowers, strong growth habit, and lustrous foliage offer great texture and vibrant colors to the garden. Camellias can be used in groupings, in shade gardens, and as informal hedges, screens, and individual specimens.

Although camellias have traditionally been considered landscape favorites for warmer climates in the United States, extensive research has produced many new, cold-hardy varieties that can be used in northern areas. The majority of these cold-hardy selections are the result of extensive work done by two scientists, Dr. William L. Ackerman and Dr. Clifford R. Parks. The Ackerman hybrids are primarily hybrids of several different species, whereas the Parks selections are hybrids and choice Japanese camellia varieties. These resilient plants flower in either fall or spring, depending on the variety chosen. The Japanese camellia varieties normally flower from early to late spring, and some of the hybrids bloom in late fall. It is important to understand that in colder climates, with shorter growing seasons, these camellias will generally not grow as large, remaining shrubby.

One key element in growing camellias successfully is the time of year they are planted. To ensure that your camellia plants become established quickly, they should be planted when weather conditions are mild and optimum for root growth. In the North camellias should be planted in spring after the harsh temperatures have subsided. The plants will develop root and top growth during the spring and summer, before the onset of winter. Camellias used outdoors in colder climates should be sited carefully, avoiding cold, windy, exposed areas of the garden. Camellias should be given north or west exposures to avoid the morning sun in winter. If sited incorrectly, camellias will be more susceptible to winter damage and leaf desiccation.

In gardens in the South, fall planting is recommended, after the harsh heat of summer has passed. In this situation the camellias will establish roots before the scorching heat of summer returns.

Camellia japonica (Japanese camellia)

There are many hardy camellia selections available, though I list just a few exceptional ones to consider when beginning your journey with this fine garden plant. These selections are most reliable in Hardiness Zones 7–9, although they will also grow in Zone 6 if properly sited.

NOTABLE VARIETIES

'April Blush'. This variety grows into a bushy plant with deep green leaves and shell pink, semidouble blooms.

'April Rose'. This compact and rather slow-growing plant has rose red double flowers. It is very floriferous and will bloom in midspring.

'April Snow'. A relatively slow-growing plant, its white double flowers provide a profuse display of color in spring.

'Kumasaka'. One of the oldest varieties of camellia, having been grown in Japan since 1695. The double blooms are red or deep rose and open late in spring.

'Lady Clare'. This variety has semidouble pink flowers.

Camellia sasanqua (Sasanqua camellia)

In addition to Japanese camellias and their hybrids, Sasanqua camellias can really brighten up the autumn with their wonderful white, pink, or red flowers. This species is generally smaller than Japanese camellia, growing 6–10 ft. tall. The plant has a finer texture than Japanese camellia, with delicate flowers and glossy leaves. It is hardy from Zones 7–9 but should be protected in northern gardens. 'Cleopatra' is a very strong grower with pink, semidouble flowers and an upright habit.

{ Cercis spp.
Redbud
Cercis canadensis (eastern redbud)

Eastern redbud is a North American native found from New England to the Southeast and Midwest. It can be spotted from a distance in groupings along highways in early spring, with its showy flowers. The deep reddish purple flower buds open to rosy pink flowers. Redbud flowers at a very young age, and as it matures, flower buds continue to bloom even on older stems and thick trunks.

As the flowers fade, smooth, glossy, bronze-colored, heart-shaped leaves unfurl, turning deep green when fully developed. The leaves usually do not offer particularly ornamental fall foliage color, although they can sometimes change to shades of yellow. As a member of the pea family, eastern redbud develops long, slender seed pods in late summer, but they are usually not particularly ornamental. Older trees can display a picturesque growth habit and rough, dark brown bark that is interesting in the winter months.

© Bruce Curtis

Bright pink flowers of redbud

Redbud in the landscape

© Vincent A. Simeone

Lustrous, heart-shaped leaves of redbud

© Vincent A. Simeone

White-flowering redbud in the landscape

Eastern redbud prefers moist, well-drained soil and full sun or partial shade. However, it is very adaptable to a wide variety of soils and light. It is at its best when located in partially shaded woodlands with rich, organic, acidic soil. A wilt disease and a stem disease called canker can be troublesome, especially on poorly sited, stressed specimens. In my experience redbud is not a particularly long-lived tree, but even so, I recommend it because of its colorful floral display and lush foliage.

Eastern redbud is very versatile and can be effectively used as a single specimen in a lawn or in small group-ings in a woodland garden among rhododendrons, azaleas, and dogwoods. It is a very fine choice as a woodland plant under the dappled light of pine trees. During regular pilgrimages to North Carolina and Georgia to collect plants, I often admired the redbuds sprinkled along Interstate 85. Hardy from Zones 4–9.

NOTABLE VARIETIES

'Alba'. This variety is truly one of the most exquisite trees in flower. It offers pure white masses of flowers and gracefully spreading branches. 'Royal White' offers larger flowers, which open slightly earlier than 'Alba'.

'Appalachian Red'. Striking, deep purple-red flower buds open to bright pink flowers—a stunning show of color in spring.

'Covey' ('Pendula'), also known as the Lavender Twist or weeping redbud. This tree offers a weeping, dwarf habit and soft pink flowers in spring. The rich, dark green, heart-shaped leaves provide a bold texture in the landscape.

'Flame' ('Plena'). This variety offers unusual double pink flowers that look like delicate rosebuds.

'Forest Pansy'. One of my favorite selections, it has deep rosy pink flowers and smooth, luxurious, deep maroon foliage that fades to greenish purple as it

Weeping redbud in flower

© Vincent A. Simeone

Deep maroon, glossy foliage of 'Forest Pansy'

matures. The new growth is simply stunning and reason alone for planting 'Forest Pansy' in the garden!

'Oklahoma'. This cultivated variety originated from a naturally occurring variety native to Texas, Oklahoma, and Mexico known as *C. canadensis* var. *texensis*. It offers deep rosy magenta flowers in spring and thick, highly glossy leaves in the summer.

'Silver Cloud'. This selection displays rosy pink flowers, followed by leaves with speckles and splashes of creamy white and pink variegation. It is an interesting accent plant in the summer landscape.

'Texas White'. Like 'Oklahoma', this is a garden variety of *C. canadensis* var. *texensis*. It offers thick, shiny foliage and milky white flowers.

Cercis chinensis (Chinese redbud)

This small tree typically has a shrubby, dense habit and is ideal for gardens with limited space. It offers a profuse show of rosy purple flowers in spring and thick, glossy, heart-shaped leaves in summer. It has an upright habit and generally grows 6–10 ft. tall, but can grow as high as 15 ft.

Chinese redbud does particularly well in warmer climates and adapts well to a variety of soil types. It is best in full sun or partial shade and moist, organic, well-drained garden soil.

NOTABLE VARIETIES

'Alba'. This attractive white-flowering form will brighten up the landscape.

'Avondale'. This variety displays stunning, deep rosy purple-pink flowers produced in great profusion along each stem. In flower it will stop garden visitors dead in their tracks with its shocking beauty.

{ *Chimonanthus praecox*
Fragrant wintersweet

Fragrant wintersweet is yet another large shrub that can be converted into a small tree with judicious pruning. This delightful winter-blooming plant typically flowers in late winter and offers a sweet fragrance at a time when not many plants are blooming in the garden. The small, cup-shaped, waxy, yellow flowers with deep reddish purple centers offer a nice display in the stark winter landscape. I have witnessed this plant flowering as early as December or January, but it flowers more reliably in late winter or early spring, when the weather is cool but not frigid. The flowers are sensitive to extreme cold temperatures, though, and may be damaged from sudden drops in temperature.

The tall, upright habit gives fragrant wintersweet the form of a small tree reaching 10–15 ft. high but usually stays smaller in northern gardens. The dark green, sharply pointed, rough-textured leaves feel like sandpaper when rubbed and turn handsome shades of yellow and green in fall.

Wintersweet is an easy plant to grow in the garden and will adapt to varying types of soils, provided there is adequate drainage. It flowers best in full sun or partial shade in a sheltered area of the garden. This plant is hardy from Zones 6–9, but in Zone 6 it should be sited in a protected area.

This winter-blooming tree is excellent as a small specimen near a walkway or patio, so the delightful fragrance can be enjoyed. In addition, branches can be cut and forced into flower indoors for a table centerpiece. Regular selective pruning to remove older, less-productive stems should be done in early spring.

NOTABLE VARIETY

'Luteus'. The beautiful golden yellow flowers have no purple coloration in the center.

{ *Chionanthus* spp.
Fringetree
Chionanthus virginicus (white fringetree)

This spring bloomer can be trained as a single- or multi-stemmed tree. It displays white, lacy, hanging flower clusters that provide a sweet fragrance. As the flowers fade, long, dark green, lustrous leaves unfurl; in the fall they turn a subdued yellow. The rounded, spreading habit accented by spring flowers is quite a show.

Lacy, white flowers of fringetree

White fringetree prefers moist, well-drained soil and full sun or partial shade. It adapts well to various soil types and levels of light exposure. Pruning at an early age to establish a strong growth habit is beneficial.

White fringetree is an excellent specimen tree and is equally effective in small groupings. It is especially useful in a shaded, woodland setting as an understory tree. Hardy from Zones 4–9.

Chionanthus retusus (Chinese fringetree)

There is an Asian fringetree species that is just as beautiful as the native American species. *Chionanthus retusus* (Chinese fringetree) is one of the most handsome flowering trees in the spring landscape. It offers dense, fleecy, fragrant white clusters of flowers that look like puffy white clouds. The dark green, rounded, glossy leaves are also quite striking. After flowering, a cluster of deep bluish fruit forms, offering additional ornamental value. The growth habit is dense and rounded, and on older specimens the bark becomes rough and deeply textured. Mature plants can range in size from 15–25 ft. tall, with a similar spread.

Chinese fringetree prefers moist, well-drained soil and full sun or partial shade. It is quite versatile, adapting to many landscape situations. It can be used as a single-specimen tree in a lawn area, in groupings, or in a woodland setting. One of the best specimens I have ever witnessed is at Wave Hill, a public garden in the Bronx, New York. Hardy from Zones 5–8.

{ *Cladrastis kentukea*
Yellowwood

This American native is found growing naturally in the southeastern United States but is also used in cultivated landscapes from the Midwest to the Northeast. It is an adaptable, medium-sized tree that offers pendulous clusters of fragrant creamy white flowers in early summer. The flower clusters hang down like long chains and resemble the blooms of wisteria. Oddly enough, this tree has the reputation of blooming heavily in alternate years, meaning that every other year you can rely on an especially heavy crop of blooms. The long, pinnately compound leaves are deep green in summer and turn variations of pale to golden yellow in the fall. In addition, the smooth gray bark is attractive, especially in the winter.

Yellowwood is quite adaptable but prefers moist, well-drained soil and full sun or partial shade. It is adaptable to soil pH and tolerates high-pH (alkaline) soil especially well.

Yellowwood is ideal as a single-specimen shade tree in a lawn area. It can reach 40–50 ft. tall, with a similar width, so it should be carefully sited in gardens with plenty of room. Hardy from Zones 4–8.

NOTABLE VARIETY

'Perkins Pink', also known as 'Rosea'. Pink flowers stand out from luxurious, dark green foliage.

{ *Clethra barbinervis*
Japanese clethra

Japanese clethra is a close relative of the shrubby, native summersweet clethra (*Clethra alnifolia*), but it grows

Deep maroon foliage and seedpods of Japanese clethra in the fall

© Vincent A. Simeone

Smooth, exfoliating bark of Japanese clethra

© Bruce Curtis

considerably taller. It offers four seasons of interest, especially in winter, displaying smooth, multicolored, exfoliating bark. The bark displays shades of gray, beige, and rich brown, which stand out in the winter landscape. In addition to the beautiful bark, Japanese clethra offers fragrant spikes of white flowers in early summer and lush, green leaves that turn red or maroon in autumn. Golden brown fruit clusters provide a beautiful contrast against the foliage.

Japanese clethra grows best in moist, organic, well-drained soil and full sun or partial shade. It prefers to be sheltered from intense wind, heat, and other harsh conditions. Eager gardeners must be patient because Japanese clethra requires a few years to become established in the landscape. Once that occurs, however, this small tree will provide unique beauty throughout all four seasons.

Japanese clethra can reach 15–20 ft. in height, making it suitable as a small specimen tree for a residential landscape. It can be used in a frontyard in a manner similar to dogwood, crabapple, or flowering cherry. Hardy from Zones 5–7.

{ *Cornus* spp.
Dogwood

There are about fifty species of dogwoods from all over the world, but few match the beauty and grace of the flowering dogwood (*Cornus florida*), also called the American dogwood. This American native has long been regarded as one of the great American flowering trees because of its showy white or pink flowers in spring. Many of us have fond memories growing up admiring the neighbor's dogwood tree that bloomed consistently

© Vincent A. Simeone
White flowering dogwood in spring

© Vincent A. Simeone
White bracts of flowering dogwood

each spring. Both the flowering dogwood and the kousa dogwood (*Cornus kousa*) offer beautiful white, four-bract flowers that are rivaled by few flowering trees. Flowering dogwood blooms before its leaves emerge in midspring, whereas kousa dogwood blooms after the leaves have unfolded and flowers appear about three weeks later than flowering dogwood. Another difference is that flowering dogwood tends to bloom more consistently as a young tree than does kousa dogwood. Although these two reliable species are best known for their flowers, they also offer interesting fall fruit and outstanding reddish purple fall foliage color. Their interesting bark, stem, and growth characteristics can be quite handsome in the winter.

The flowering dogwood matures into a dense, rounded tree that will eventually develop rough, gray bark resembling alligator skin. The bark's coarse texture makes an interesting backdrop for the subtle display of the smooth, rounded, gray flower buds. Meanwhile, established kousa dogwoods typically exhibit beautiful exfoliating (flaking) bark with shades of tan, gray, and brown. The bark's camouflage appearance is most prominent in winter, especially on older trees that have developed the picturesque growth habit of thick, strong trunks and branches.

Cornus florida (flowering dogwood)

Flowering dogwoods are undoubtedly among the most popular and revered of all flowering trees. There is nothing quite like a dogwood in spring displaying masses of white or pink blossoms. The showy white or pink parts of the blossom are not petals; they are bracts, which are essentially modified leaves that surround the relatively insignificant flower cluster. The small, round, and greenish yellow cluster of flowers offers little ornamental value, and it is most often the showy outer bracts that are admired. Once the bracts fall off and the true flowers are pollinated, a glossy, rounded fruit will develop, ripening to deep red in the autumn. The fruit is devoured by many species of birds.

Although flowering dogwoods are mainly known for their exquisite flowers (bracts), their excellent red fall foliage color, interesting fruit display, beautiful bark texture, and picturesque growth habit offer four-season interest. Over the past few decades many exciting new dogwood varieties and hybrids have been developed with improved disease resistance, aesthetic value, and landscape function.

Ideally, flowering dogwood should be sited in an area of the garden with the dappled light provided from conifers or high canopy of a finely textured overstory forest. Flowering dogwood performs best in moist, acidic, well-drained soil amended with generous amounts of organic matter.

American dogwood is known to be susceptible to several diseases, such as dogwood anthracnose and powdery mildew. Dogwood anthracnose can be devastating under certain environmental conditions. A tree sited in dense shade with little air circulation is more susceptible to anthracnose and other foliar pests. Flowering dogwood is less likely to fall prey to these ailments if sited correctly: in a partially shaded area of the garden with morning sun and plenty of air circulation. It may be sited in full sun, provided that adequate supplemental irrigation and moist, well-drained soil and mulch are provided.

Flowering dogwood is an excellent single specimen in a front lawn or in small groupings as part of a woodland planting. No matter how you use it in the landscape, nothing says spring like a flowering dogwood. Hardy from Zones 5–7.

NOTABLE VARIETIES

There are white- and pink-flowering types of flowering dogwood. The pink form is a naturally occurring variety, written *Cornus florida* var. *rubra*. Here are a few good selections of both pink and white cultivars of flowering dogwood.

'Cherokee Brave'. A superior selection of pink dogwood, this one has attractive deep reddish pink bracts and dark green foliage. In the fall the foliage turns a deep shade of reddish maroon.

© Vincent A. Simeone

Pink flowering dogwood in spring

© Vincent A. Simeone

'Cherokee Brave' dogwood bracts

© Bruce Curtis

Pink bracts of flowering dogwood

'Cherokee Chief'. This older variety has deep pink bracts.

'Cherokee Princess'. A beautiful white form of flowering dogwood, it has large white bracts and dark green foliage and seems to be fairly resistant to dogwood anthracnose.

'Cloud Nine'. An excellent, cold-hardy variety with showy white bracts, it flowers profusely at a very early age and develops a spreading habit as it matures.

'Eddie's White Wonder'. This unique hybrid has exceptionally large white bracts, which offer an outstandingly bold display in spring.

'Plena'. Although there are several "double" varieties, 'Plena' is considered the general term for varieties offering double white bracts, which provide a ruffled look to the flowers.

'Spring Grove'. This select variety offers large, 5 in. wide white bracts in spring. It is also known to display a heavy fruit set.

'Welchii'. This variegated form offers combinations of green, cream, and pink in the foliage. Bracts are white, and fall foliage color is an outstanding reddish purple. It performs best if sited in partial shade, protected from the hot afternoon sun.

Cornus kousa (kousa dogwood)

Native to Japan, China, and Korea, the kousa dogwood is similar to the American flowering dogwood in some ways, but quite different in many others. For example, unlike *Cornus florida*, kousa dogwood flowers after its leaves emerge in late spring. It is also quite resistant to dogwood anthracnose, which has devastated thousands of flowering dogwoods.

Kousa dogwood has many aesthetically pleasing attributes. Although it is most well known for its showy white bracts in early summer, kousa dogwood displays lustrous green foliage; a fleshy, reddish orange fruit, which ripens in the early autumn; reddish maroon fall foliage; a picturesque vase-shaped growth habit; and multicolored, exfoliating bark.

In late spring small chartreuse, pointed bracts form along each stem like soldiers at attention. As they mature through the early summer, the bracts enlarge and turn pure white. Kousa flowers last about a month, fading as the hottest summer weather approaches. As the flowers fade, the white bracts often become tinged with pink before falling to the ground.

As summer progresses, a small, rounded green fruit develops into a reddish fruit about the size of a quar-

Dense, white bracts of kousa dogwood

© Bruce Curtis

Kousa dogwood in the landscape

© Bruce Curtis

The exfoliating bark of kousa dogwood

© Bruce Curtis

Kousa dogwood in the fall

© Bruce Curtis

© Vincent A. Simeone

Rounded, fleshy fruit of kousa dogwood

© Vincent A. Simeone

Pickles waiting for a tasty treat

ter. In addition to being ornamental, this fruit is edible. Several years ago I observed my dog Pickles busily foraging on the ground with delight, devouring the sweet kousa fruit. This did not surprise me, because Pickles has the reputation of being a nonselective eater. But I was pleasantly surprised to learn that the fruit, when fully ripened, is quite tasty, although I suspect it may be an acquired taste for some. Each fall my faithful canine companion and I can be found feasting on this unusual delicacy. Birds and small animals, such as chipmunks, squirrels, and rabbits, also find this food source tasty.

Unlike many other flowering trees, kousa dogwood offers ornamental interest even in the fall and winter months. During the fall the leaves turn brilliant shades of red or purple, and as the leaves drop, the multicolored, exfoliating bark is revealed. This beautiful bark feature and kousa dogwood's layered, vase-shaped growth habit are additional reasons, besides the flowers and fruit, to plant this worthy landscape tree. As it matures, kousa dogwood becomes increasingly picturesque. All these attributes make kousa dogwood one of the best flowering trees for the home garden.

Kousa dogwood is quite adaptable in the landscape, but it thrives in moist, well-drained soil and full sun or partial shade. It does best in rich, organic garden soil with adequate moisture during the hot summer months. Kousa dogwood is very effective as a single specimen in a lawn area or in small groupings on both residential and commercial sites. Placing kousa dogwood along a walkway or near a patio should be avoided because of the fleshy and potentially messy fruit, which ripens in the fall. I have also witnessed kousa dogwood thriving in a shady woodland setting among rhododendrons, azaleas, hollies, and shade-loving perennials. Hardy from Zones 5–7.

NOTABLE VARIETIES

'Gold Star'. This variegated variety offers beautiful white flowers but is more often grown for its colorful foliage, which displays golden yellow blotches in the centers of the dark green leaves.

'Lustgarten Weeping'. This unusual form has a strong weeping habit. The lustrous green leaves and graceful habit make this plant a standout specimen in the landscape. 'Weaver's Weeping' is another weeping form that is very floriferous, with showy white flowers.

'Milky Way'. This exceptionally floriferous form provides a stunning display, with masses of beautiful white blooms along each stem. The entire tree is smothered with clouds of white at bloom time.

'Satomi'. This variety, also found under the name 'Rosabella', has beautiful deep pink bracts and glossy green foliage. In 1999 I witnessed a small specimen in full bloom in the garden of Dr. Sun Yat-sen in Vancouver, British Columbia. This small but heavily flowering tree was simply breathtaking. It was truly one of the most memorable flowering trees I have ever witnessed in bloom. In cooler, less humid climates the pink color tends to be more intense. When not in flower, the foliage alone is a beautiful sight.

'Summer Stars'. This select variety was discovered in 1972 by the late, great horticulturist Peter Costich of Long Island. This variety offers long-lasting flowers

that turn pink as they fade with age in the late summer or early autumn.

'Wolf Eyes'. Here's another variegated kousa dogwood, with foliage displaying deep green centers and creamy white margins.

© Vincent A. Simeone

'Satomi' in bloom

© Vincent A. Simeone

'Summer Stars' fading to blush pink in late summer

Rutgers hybrid dogwoods

In addition to the popular flowering dogwood and the kousa dogwood, there are several hybrids that are excellent flowering trees for the home garden. Since 1965, Dr. Elwin Orton of Rutgers University in New Jersey has been hybridizing several species to develop the Rutgers hybrid dogwoods. From his research, six cultivated varieties known as the Stellar series were developed. More recently, two more hybrids have been developed as part of the Jersey Star series. These hybrids are primarily offspring of *C. florida* and *C. kousa* varieties, although other species have been used, as well. These crosses offer the best aesthetic attributes of both species as well as the disease resistance of *C. kousa*, being quite resistant to powdery mildew and dogwood anthracnose.

In addition, Rutgers hybrid trees typically bloom before *C. florida* finishes blooming but after *C. kousa* starts, bridging the gap in bloom time. However, enthusiastic gardeners should be patient with these exceptional flowering trees. Newly planted hybrids take several years to become established and flower heavily in the landscape. They are undoubtedly well worth the wait, because they get better with age. Once established, these hardy trees will perform admirably year after year, providing beautiful flowers, lush green summer foliage, and brilliant reddish maroon fall foliage color. These hybrids are functional, culturally adaptable, and aesthetically pleasing in the landscape.

NOTABLE VARIETIES

Over the last ten years, Rutgers hybrids have gained in popularity, and now they can be found in local garden centers and nurseries. Quite a few popular cultivars combine the best of several excellent species, making them ideal for the home garden. Here are a few exceptional selections that will add beauty and function in the landscape.

Aurora ('Rutban'). Plants of this hybrid are very vigorous and erect in habit but uniformly quite wide from top to bottom. They are very dense bloomers.

Constellation ('Rutcan'). Plants of this hybrid are erect in habit, are much more vigorous than typical kousa dogwoods, and do not exhibit the vase-shaped habit of young kousas, this hybrid being more fully branched low to the ground. The bracts are more open than Aurora's.

Celestial ('Rutdan'). This variety offers large white flowers with rounded bracts and excellent resistance to anthracnose. This upright tree develops a rounded to vase-shaped growth habit and will reach 20–30 ft. in height. The bracts are white with a tinge of green and

New flowers of Celestial unfurling in spring

form a deep cup early in the season. As they mature, the bracts flatten out and become fully white.

Ruth Ellen ('Rutlan'). Plants of this hybrid are similar to plants of *C. florida* as far as general growth habit: lower and spreading, rather than upright. Established specimens in the landscape will generally reach 20 ft. tall and 25 ft. wide and will be densely branched close to the ground.

Stardust ('Rutfan'). This hybrid is more like *C. florida* than *C. kousa* in general outline and horizontal spreading habit. This tree offers branches low to the ground and will flower heavily.

Stellar Pink ('Rutgan'). This is the only pink variety of the hybrid dogwoods, offering a light to blush pink flower and lustrous dark green foliage.

Starlight. This hybrid of *Cornus kousa* and *C. nuttallii* exhibits the vigorous nature and large white bracts of *C. nuttallii* and the dark, glossy green foliage and disease and insect resistance of *C. kousa*. Plants of this hybrid grow very vigorously and become upright, uniformly wide, and densely branched.

Venus. This is the latest Rutgers introduction and one of the most spectacular. A hybrid between *Cornus kousa* and *C. nuttallii*, this flowering tree offers exceptionally large, white floral bracts, making, 5 in. wide blooms that will stop you cold in your tracks. This hybrid is also distinguished by its superior winter hardiness, good tolerance of drought conditions, and high resistance to powdery mildew and dogwood anthracnose. Venus grows very vigorously, with upright branches forming a rounded canopy and branching low to the ground.

© Vincent A. Simeone

Large white blooms of Venus

Other dogwoods

Besides the more common species and hybrid dogwoods discussed, several lesser-known species are becoming popular in American landscapes. Varieties of these species have been commonly used in Europe for many years for their foliage, form, and flowers. *Cornus alternifolia* (pagoda dogwood) and *C. controversa* (giant dogwood) are two somewhat obscure species that offer beautiful dark green foliage, layered growth habit, and unusual flat-topped, creamy white flowers called cymes. *C. controversa* tends to possess noticeably larger foliage, flowers, fruit clusters, and overall size, but both species generally grow to about 20–30 ft. The growth pattern, even on young trees, is layered, with lateral branches growing in a horizontal pattern, a beautiful, picturesque growth habit that only improves with age. The dark green, lustrous leaves can turn shades of purple in fall, along with clusters of reddish black berries.

Although these species are difficult to find in commerce, the variegated forms of both are becoming more available to the gardener who seeks them out. *Cornus alternifolia* 'Argentea' and *C. controversa* 'Variegata' offer leaves with various combinations of green, creamy white, and pink in the foliage. *C. controversa* 'Variegata' is also called the wedding cake tree because its branch layering is typically very pronounced, like tiers on a wedding cake. These species' interesting habits and reddish purple stems make them attractive trees in winter.

These small to medium-sized trees are excellent accents in a partially shaded landscape. For example, in a woodland setting, they provide a splash of color against a dark green background. *C. alternifolia* is hardy from Zones 3–7, and *C. controversa* is hardy from Zones 5–7 and possibly 4 with protection.

© Vincent A. Simeone

Cornus controversa 'Variegata', with its tiered branching habit

{ *Cornus mas*
Cornelian cherry

This remarkably adaptable early-flowering tree displays several unique ornamental characteristics. The entire tree displays a warm glow before any other flowering tree has even broken dormancy. Small bouquets of bright yellow flowers open in late winter or early spring and persist for several weeks. The glossy green leaves and oval, cherry red fruit in summer are also very attractive. The fruit is preferred by birds and other wildlife and can also be used to make preserves.

Golden yellow flowers of Cornelian cherry

© Bruce Curtis

© Vincent A. Simeone

Cornelian cherry in bloom

In addition to early- and midseason interest, Cornelian cherry is also beautiful during the cold winter months, displaying a rough, exfoliating, rich brown bark. The thin, green stems and rounded flower buds also add subtle interest. Cornelian cherry will grow 20–25 ft. tall, with a slightly smaller spread.

Cornelian cherry is a tough landscape tree, tolerating poor soil and exposed sites, heat, and drought, but it thrives in moist, well-drained soil and full sun or partial shade. It can be very useful as a single specimen, in raised planters, or in small groupings. Hardy from Zones 4–7, but it tolerates Zone 8 with specific siting.

Cornus officinalis (Japanese cornel dogwood) is very similar to cornelian cherry, but it typically flowers a bit earlier, and the fruit ripens later in the season.

NOTABLE VARIETIES

'Aurea'. Bright golden foliage makes this variety an excellent accent plant for a partially shaded area of the garden.

'Elegantissima'. This variety displays combinations of green and gold, accented with pink tones on new foliage.

'Golden Glory'. This variety offers an upright growth habit and a profusion of golden yellow flowers.

'Variegata'. Leaves are accented with a bright creamy white border.

{ *Corylus colurna*
Turkish filbert

Turkish filbert, also known as hazel, is far from what would be considered a traditional flowering tree. This upright deciduous tree can reach 40–50 ft. tall, with half the spread. In early spring, 2–3 in. long, brown, male flowers known as catkins dangle from the tree. Although this effect is not very colorful, like a dogwood or crabap-

© Vincent A. Simeone

Drooping catkins of Turkish filbert

ple in full bloom, it provides quite an interesting, graceful display. The dark green leaves turn shades of yellow to reddish purple in the fall. The tan to gray-brown bark becomes rough and flaky with age and adds winter interest to the landscape. The fruit, a hazelnut, is edible, but it is often snatched up by squirrels and other wildlife.

Turkish filbert is an extremely adaptable tree, tolerating heat, drought, and cold climates. It prefers full sun or partial shade and moist, well-drained soil but is remarkably adaptable to various soil types and soil pH. Young trees require a few years to become established in the landscape.

Turkish filbert is a rather difficult tree to find in commerce but is a great addition to the garden. It can be used as a single-specimen tree in a lawn area or in harsh, exposed sites and could be useful as an urban tree for large commercial sites. Hardy from Zones 4–7.

{ *Cotinus obovatus*
American smoketree

The American smoketree, a small tree growing 25–30 ft. tall, offers large, blue-green, lustrous foliage. The stunning foliage turns brilliant shades of yellow, orange, crimson red, and purple in autumn. Puffs of tiny greenish yellow flowers change to pink with age in the midsummer months. The flower clusters range from 6 to 10 in. long and resemble puffs of smoke, hence the common name. This upright tree displays a broad, rounded habit and rough, gray bark, which is most noticeable in the winter.

American smoketree prefers well-drained soil and is quite happy in hot, dry locations. Moist, well-drained garden soil is also acceptable, though. Full sun is preferred, although the tree will adapt to partial shade.

American smoketree is ideal as a single specimen in a lawn area or in groupings. It has great potential in urban conditions or near the seashore. Hardy from Zones 4–8.

Cotinus coggygria (smokebush), a more commonly found species, typically grows much smaller than American smoketree but can be trained into a multi-stemmed tree to 15 ft. tall. 'Grace' is a hybrid offering smooth, pinkish red foliage that matures to blue-green in summer. Its leaves turn a deep orange or red in the fall. 'Velvet Cloak', one of the best purple-leaf varieties, has leaves emerging a deep maroon and, as they mature, change to purple-green. Fall foliage color is a rich reddish purple.

{ *Crataegus* spp.
Hawthorn

Hawthorns are beautiful, durable flowering trees that tolerate hot, dry, exposed locations as well as urban conditions. The clusters of white or deep pink flowers develop in the spring. The blossoms are followed by reddish orange, apple-shaped fruits that are typically less than 1 in. across. The fruits often persist on the branches into the winter. Hawthorns are equipped with very sharp thorns, so the gardener must carefully site them in the landscape.

Crataegus phaenopyrum (Washington hawthorn)

The is one of our best native hawthorns because of its adaptability, durability, and multiple ornamental qualities. In the spring, bouquets of white flowers are high-

© Vincent A. Simeone

Large thorns of hawthorn

lighted against the lustrous green leaves that are similar to maple leaves, but smaller. The fall is one of the best seasons for this flowering tree because the foliage turns brilliant shades of red and the clusters of glossy, red fruit ripen, the latter persisting through the winter months. Washington hawthorn offers a dense, oval to rounded growth habit and will reach 20–25 ft. high and wide. Older specimens display rough, flaking, reddish brown bark.

Washington hawthorn prefers moist, well-drained soil and full sun but is remarkably adaptable to soil types, soil pH, and shade. It will tolerate dry, sandy soil; heavy, clay soil; heat; drought; pollution; and even seashore conditions.

Washington hawthorn, although very popular as a tree for parks and urban settings, can also serve as an ornamental in residential settings. But beware! This tree does possess 1–3 in. long thorns, so it must be sited carefully in a low-traffic area where it can be admired from afar. It is very effective as a single specimen or in groupings in a lawn area. Hardy from Zones 3–8.

Crataegus crus-galli var. inermis
(thornless cockspur hawthorn)

This naturally occurring variety's name, *inermis*, means "unarmed," hinting at the tree's status as a thornless alternative to the Washington hawthorn. It offers a broad, dense habit; smooth, glossy green leaves, and white clusters of flowers in midspring. In the fall the leaves turn brilliant shades of crimson red, bronze, and purple. Large, reddish orange fruit form in clusters and will persist much of the winter. The dense, irregular branches catch freshly fallen snow, offering a beautiful aesthetic display in winter.

Cockspur hawthorn prefers moist, well-drained soil but, like most species of hawthorns, will adapt to almost any landscape situation, including poor, compacted soil, heat, and drought. It performs best in full sun but will also do well in partial shade.

Because this variety is thornless, siting in high-traffic areas is not a concern. This flowering tree is ideal as a single specimen or in small groupings. Hardy from Zones 3–7.

Crataegus viridis 'Winter King'
(Winter King hawthorn)

This beautiful tree offers showy clusters of white flowers in spring, an abundant crop of persistent orange-red fruit in the fall and winter, and grayish green stems in winter. On older trees the bark exfoliates, exposing shades of gray, green, beige, and cinnamon brown

underneath. The lovely vase-shaped growth habit and glossy, dark green summer foliage add to the beauty of Winter King hawthorn. Although not one of the primary ornamental features of this tree, the foliage will turn golden yellow with accents of reddish maroon.

The Winter King hawthorn, like most hawthorns, is quite adaptable to most types of soil, heat, drought,

© Vincent A. Simeone

Flowers and foliage of Winter King hawthorn

© Vincent A. Simeone

Reddish orange fruit of Winter King hawthorn

and various degrees of light exposure. It does prefers moist, well-drained soil and full sun. Although many species of hawthorns are susceptible to diseases, 'Winter King' is quite resistant.

'Winter King' hawthorn is an excellent small tree for a lawn area or in a small grouping, being truly one of the best hawthorns for fruit display, winter interest, and pest resistance. Hardy from Zones 4–7.

Davidia involucrata
Dove tree

Dove tree, also known as handkerchief tree, is truly one of the most unique and breathtaking trees in flower. In spring established trees produce large, 5–6 in. long white bracts, which hang on either side of a small, rounded flower. The white bracts wave in the wind like the wings of a dove. The dark green, lustrous leaves form a dense canopy during the summer months. Young trees have an upright, pyramidal habit, which will develop into a more broad, rounded shape over time. During the winter months, the rough, orange-brown bark becomes very prominent.

This exquisite tree is native to the mountains of southwest China. It was given its botanical name in honor of

The great plant explorer E. H. Wilson once said about dove tree:

"To my mind *Davidia involucrata* is at once the most interesting and beautiful of all trees of the north-temperate flora. . . .

The flowers and their attendant bracts are pendulous on fairly long stalks, and when stirred by the slightest breeze they resemble huge Butterflies hovering amongst the trees."

Dove tree in flower

© Vincent A. Simeone

Dove tree flower up close

© Vincent A. Simeone

French missionary Fr. Armand David (1826–1900), who first reported the tree in 1869. He spoke of large white flowers hanging like handkerchiefs (or fluttering like doves, depending on the weather) from the branches.

Dove tree prefers moist, well-drained soil and full sun or partial shade. It should be sited somewhere in the garden where it has plenty of room because it can reach 20–40 ft. tall. It will establish rather quickly but needs a few years to flower reliably.

Dove tree is one of the most exquisite specimen flowering trees and is ideal in a lawn area or woodland garden. You will no doubt be the talk of the neighborhood when this tree is in full bloom. Hardy from Zones 5–7; in Zone 5 it does need some protection and should be sited in a sheltered location.

Franklinia alatamaha
Franklinia, Ben Franklin tree

Franklinia, like so many species of native trees, has an interesting story to tell. It was first discovered by the famous botanist and plant collector John Bartram in 1770 along the Altamaha River in southeastern Georgia. The tree was named *Franklinia alatamaha* in honor of Bartram's great friend Benjamin Franklin, hence the common name Ben Franklin tree. Franklinia has not been seen in the wild since 1803.

Franklinia is a very beautiful tree offering four seasons of interest, with late-summer blossoms, striking fall foliage, and winter bark interest. The franklinia tree reaches a height of 10–20 ft. It is typically found as a multistemmed tree offering white, fragrant flowers in late summer and early fall. The flowers have bright yellow centers and look similar to *Camellia* and *Stewartia* flowers because all are in the tea family. The dark green leaves turn brilliant shades of orange, crimson red, and maroon. This flowering tree, though impressive in flower, is also one of the best for fall foliage color. Even the bark is interesting on franklinia, dark gray or brown with silvery white stripes—quite attractive during the winter months.

Franklinia does have a reputation for being difficult to grow. To ensure success, proper site selection and careful preplanting preparation are very important.

Franklinia needs excellent soil drainage and acidic soil rich in organic matter. Poorly drained, heavy soil will undoubtedly spell doom for this finicky tree. Although franklinia tolerates full sun as well as dense shade, it prefers the dappled light created by the overhead canopy of tall trees. Mulch 1–2 in. thick will also be beneficial to franklinia because it will keep roots cool and reduce water loss in the soil during the hot summer months.

Showy white franklinia blooms

© Bruce Curtis

Franklinia is gaining in popularity, thanks to the dedicated work of Bartram's Garden in Philadelphia, Pennsylvania. Franklinia is treasured by gardeners who are enticed by its delicate beauty and fortunate enough to have the proper growing environment to accommodate its cultural demands. Franklinia is an excellent woodland tree for a shade garden. It can be effectively used as a single specimen or in small groupings. Hardy from Zones 5–8.

Halesia tetraptera
Carolina silverbell

This medium-sized tree can be a delightful addition to any garden. Its best feature is the dangling, white, bell-shaped flowers, which line up along each stem like chimes in spring. The summer foliage is dark green and rarely displays any noticeable fall color. *Halesia* is quite noticeable during the winter months, though, with gray, brown, and black colored bark that forms ridges and can develop into flat plates on the main trunks. This typically happens on older specimens. The younger stems are also gray-brown with silvery white streaks but are smoother than those on the older branches. This underutilized flowering tree offers a rounded to oval growth habit and can be grown as a single- or multitrunk tree. Established trees will grow 30 ft. or more in height, with an equal spread.

This southeastern native prefers moist, well-drained, acidic soil and full sun or partial shade. It can grow in

Dangling, white, bell-shaped flowers of silverbell

© Vincent A. Simeone

full sun but should be sited in moist, rich soil and may need to be irrigated in times of drought.

Silverbell is ideal as a single specimen or in a woodland setting, but it can also be used in a sunny lawn area, provided adequate moisture is available. Hardy from Zones 5–8, and possibly 9 with specific siting.

NOTABLE VARIETY

'Rosea'. This striking pink-flowering variety offers a range of color from blush to rich pink flowers in spring. Flower color and size are quite variable, depending on environmental conditions.

Halesia diptera var. *magniflora* is a select variety of *Halesia* that offers exceptionally large flowers in spring. The beautiful white flowers are up to 1⅓ in. long, noticeably larger than any other species or variety of silverbell. This outstanding spring-flowering tree really makes a statement.

Heptacodium miconioides
Seven-son flower

This extraordinary Asian species is one of the most uniquely beautiful woody plants available to the passionate garden collector. Although seven-son flower is considered a four-season plant, it is undoubtedly at its best from late summer through the fall and into the winter season. Lustrous, dark green leaves with pronounced veins cover the plant in summer, accented by small, creamy white flowers in late summer. After the petals fade, the calyx, the outermost part of the flower, remains and turns deep red. The calyces, collectively clustered at the end of every stem, are quite a show in the fall. Seven-son flower is also interesting in the winter, with its light tan to silvery gray, peeling bark and strong, upright growth habit, which improves with age.

© Bruce Curtis

Showy red calyces of seven-son flower

Seven-son flower can be trained as a dense, large shrub or as an upright small tree. It does best in full sun or partial shade and moist, well-drained soil; it does not perform well in dense shade and poorly drained soils. It should be pruned only to develop a few strong main stems.

Seven-son flower is best when used as a single specimen or in a small grouping. When trained as a small tree, it will reach 12–15 ft. tall, with half the spread. Hardy from Zones 4–8.

Silvery gray bark of seven-son flower

{ *Hibiscus syriacus*
Rose of Sharon

Rose of Sharon is one of the most beloved old-fashioned flowering shrubs in American gardens. I have fond childhood memories of rose of Sharon flowering profusely in my grandparents' garden on Long Island. Even though rose of Sharon is usually grown as a dense shrub, it can also be trained as a small, upright tree. The showy white, pink, or red flowers, which resemble those of the tropical hibiscuses, emerge in mid- to late summer and offer a colorful, somewhat exotic look well into the fall. Rose of Sharon can develop a dense, vase-shaped or upright growth habit to 12 ft. tall, but it is typically found in the 8–10 ft. tall range.

Rose of Sharon is fast growing and will respond well to pruning. The ends of the branches can be pruned back in early spring while the plant is still dormant. Besides shaping and maintaining plant habit, this encourages a healthy batch of summer flowers. However, this pruning is not typically needed every year.

Rose of Sharon prefers well-drained, moist soil but will also tolerate poor soil. It will tolerate heat, drought, and infertile soil but does not perform well in soggy or poorly drained soil. For best results rose of Sharon should be sited in full sun or partial shade in an open, airy part of the garden. Although rose of Sharon is prone to several pest problems, this does not seem to discourage it from flowering consistently every year. Rose of Sharon will develop a healthy crop of fruit and disperse seed throughout the garden. Often seedlings can be found germinating in every nook and cranny of the garden. Few varieties produce little or no viable seed, and it is wise to choose sterile varieties, such as 'Diana', for this reason.

Rose of Sharon is an excellent small flowering tree that can be effective as a single specimen or in groupings. I have seen a grouping of plants in a straight line along a property line, and the effect was quite attractive. Rose of Sharon can make an interesting lawn tree in a garden with limited space. Hardy from Zones 5–8, and possibly 9 with specific siting.

NOTABLE VARIETIES

'Blue Bird'. This unusual selection offers a violet-blue flower with a dark red center.

'Diana'. A prolific bloomer, its large, pure white flowers will brighten up the landscape.

Large, pure white flowers of 'Diana'

'Helene'. This variety offers a white flower with a deep maroon center.

{ *Hydrangea paniculata*
Panicle hydrangea

Like rose of Sharon, panicle hydrangeas can double as large shrubs and as small single-stemmed trees, depending on how they are maintained. These beautiful late-season bloomers offer rounded or pyramidal panicles of white flowers in late summer and early fall. The 6–8 in. long flowers are not affected by soil pH (unlike some other hydrangeas) and will eventually change to pink as they age. The medium-green leaves will often display tinges of yellow, red, or purple in the fall. This plant can vary in size but usually grows as a tall, upright shrub with graceful, arching branches. It can easily reach 10 ft. or more in height.

Panicle hydrangea thrives in rich, moist, well-drained garden soil but is very adaptable to various soil types. Full sun or partial shade is preferable, as too much shade will reduce flower production. Panicle hydrangea blooms on the current season's growth, so it should be pruned in winter or early spring to stimulate new growth. This does not need to be done every year.

Because of its size, panicle hydrangea is suitable as a small specimen tree in a lawn and is also functional as an informal hedge, screen, or background plant in a shrub border. I have also seen this shrub used very effectively in decorative containers and urns. A very cold-hardy species, it grows from Hardiness Zones 3–8.

Panicle hydrangea in the fall

NOTABLE VARIETIES

'Grandiflora', also known as the peegee hydrangea. This is a very old, common variety with large, white flowers to 12 in. long.

'Kyushu'. A vigorous, upright-growing tree that produces large quantities of pure white flowers at an early age.

'Limelight'. A fairly recent introduction, its large panicles of flowers are a striking chartreuse green when first emerging, changing to pure white with age. This very fast grower flowers at an early age.

'Pink Diamond'. The interesting white flowers change to a rich pink color with age.

'Tardiva'. This late bloomer has showy, white, cone-shaped flower panicles lasting well into the fall season.

'Unique'. This variety offers enormous flowers in profusion. The flowers are broad at the base and bluntly rounded at the tip.

Koelreuteria paniculata
Golden raintree

When most flowering trees have finished blooming, golden raintree is just getting started. This versatile, adaptable tree is one of only a few that flowers in midsummer. The bright yellow flowers form long, loose panicles that are quite a contrast to the long, dark green, pinnately compound leaves. After the flowers finish, papery, greenish yellow seed capsules form, turning golden brown with age. Often these seedpods will persist into the winter season. Each capsule contains small, round seeds, and a gardener should beware that in the spring unwanted seedlings may germinate throughout the garden.

© Bruce Curtis

Golden raintree in the landscape

© Vincent A. Simeone

Flowers of golden raintree

© Bruce Curtis

Papery seed capsules of golden raintree

This fast-growing tree will reach 30–40 ft. tall and wide. It is very adaptable to soil types, heat, and drought and is also tolerant of pests. For best results plant golden raintree in full sun or partial shade and well-drained, moist soil.

Golden raintree is an excellent single-specimen tree for a lawn area or near a patio, or in a small grouping in a commercial setting. It has also been used as a street tree because of its adaptability and modest size. Hardy from Zones 5–8.

Koelreuteria bipinnata, also known as the Chinese flametree, is similar in size and most other characteristics to the golden raintree, but it has a rosy pink, lanternlike seedpod. I believe it is most beautiful when the seed pods form. In addition, the long, compound leaves are not serrated like *K. paniculata*'s.

NOTABLE VARIETY

'September'. A later-blooming variety flowering in late summer and early autumn.

{ *Laburnum* x *watereri* }
Goldenchain tree

Golden chaintree is one of those flowering trees that are so beautiful in spring that we overlook the fact that it is interesting only at that time of year. The best way to describe goldenchain tree in flower: simply stunning! The long, chainlike, golden yellow flower clusters resem-

© Vincent A. Simeone

Long, chainlike flower racemes of goldenchain tree

ble wisteria racemes. The flowers have a slight fragrance. This feature will last several weeks before fading.

Once the tree has finished blooming, it fades into the landscape, going unnoticed until the following spring. The habit is upright when young and spreading and somewhat rounded with age and will reach 15–20 ft. tall. The younger branches offer a noticeable olive green color, especially in winter. The small, trifolate leaves are medium to deep green in summer and offer no significant fall color.

Goldenchain tree in the landscape

© Vincent A. Simeone

Goldenchain tree is best suited for cool, moist climates, such as Europe and the Pacific Northwest of the United States. It does not perform as well in the warm, humid climates of the northeastern, southeastern, or midwestern United States. It is otherwise hardy from Zones 5–7. Goldenchain tree prefers moist, rich, organic, acidic soil and full sun or partial shade.

Goldenchain tree is an excellent small tree for spring color and can be used as a single specimen or in groupings. It is probably most impressive in an allee, with trees lining a walkway or garden path. Barnsley House, the garden of the late English gardener Rosemary Verey, features a goldenchain tree walk that glows with color when in bloom. This somewhat short-lived tree offering only one season of interest is undoubtedly worth the effort.

NOTABLE VARIETY

'Vossii'. This variety has a denser growth habit and long, chainlike flower clusters up to 2 ft. in length.

Lagerstroemia spp.
Crape myrtles
Lagerstroemia indica (crape myrtle)

Crape myrtle is a well-known flowering shrub or small tree with beautiful papery, colorful flowers in the summer. It is found extensively in gardens in the southeastern United States, where it is used in a variety of landscape situations. Its flowers range in color from white to pink to deep red. The flowers often persist into fall, followed by rounded, green fruit that looks like small clusters of grapes before ripening. This fast-

Crape myrtle flowers

Upright habit of crape myrtle

growing woody plant also displays exquisite smooth, multicolored bark, which offers interest year-round. The outer layer of bark flakes off the trunk, exposing combinations of brown, beige, or gray underneath.

Crape myrtle is a very adaptable tree or large shrub, thriving in hot, sunny locations in the garden. It does best in moist, well-drained soil but is very tolerant of poor, dry soil and heavy, clay soil. Soil drainage is very important and directly relates to the success of crape myrtle. Winter fertilization will help increase flower production and vigor.

Because crape myrtle blooms occur on the current season's growth, pruning right after the blooms fade may encourage a second flush of flowers. This technique is more effective in warmer climates with mild, extended growing seasons. In addition, wispy sucker growth from the base of the plant should be removed. If considerable pruning is needed, selective pruning while the plant is dormant in late winter will produce good results. Pruning large plants back to very thick stems or main trunks should be avoided, since that technique will often cause a flush of long, pliable, weak stems. Instead, the canopy can be thinned and top growth cut back to branches no thicker than your pinky finger.

Several species and varieties of crape myrtle can be grown as small flowering trees. Certain varieties of *Lagerstroemia indica* and *L. faurei* are ideal for this. To train crape myrtle as a small tree, prune off any young, spindly, or thin branches from the lower part of the plant, leaving several strong, main stems.

Crape myrtle (*L. indica*) is hardy from Zones 6–9 but does benefit from a sheltered location in colder climates. A light layer of mulch or pine straw around the base of your crape myrtles will help retain soil moisture and reduce soil temperature fluctuations.

Crape myrtle is a wonderful small flowering tree that can be used as a single specimen or in groupings. It is excellent in a lawn area or near a patio.

NOTABLE VARIETIES

'Lipan'. An interesting variety with lavender flowers and near white to beige bark, this intermediate form can grow 15–20 ft.

'Natchez'. A beautiful, large-growing variety with pure white flowers and cinnamon brown bark, 'Natchez' is excellent as a small tree for a home landscape, provided adequate room is available.

'Tuscarora'. Attractive dark coral pink flowers are a nice contrast to the light brown, smooth bark.

Lagerstroemia faurei (Japanese crape myrtle)

Japanese crape myrtle offers a beautiful vase-shaped growth habit, a fluted trunk base, and stunning reddish brown and beige bark. The bark interest is equal to that of *Stewartia*. Japanese crape myrtle can reach 20 or more ft. in height and is an outstanding medium-sized tree for the home garden. Like *L. indica*, *L. faurei* is hardy from Zones 6–9.

© Vincent A. Simeone

Beautiful bark of Japanese crape myrtle

'Fantasy' and 'Townhouse' are two excellent varieties offering white summer flowers and stunning bark interest. These trees have wowed me several times at the J. C. Raulston Arboretum in Raleigh, North Carolina.

{ *Maackia amurensis*
Amur maackia

Maackia is a rather obscure tree that is often overlooked by growers, landscape architects, and gardeners—and should not be. This medium-sized tree offers an upright, rounded growth habit reaching 20–30 ft. tall. In the spring the pinnately compound leaves emerge a grayish green, maturing to rich, dark green. *Maackia* does not offer any appreciable fall foliage color. In midsummer upright clusters of fragrant white flowers emerge; they persist for several weeks. Flowers smell like a freshly mown lawn. The peeling bark ranges from amber to dark brown and is quite attractive in winter.

Amur maackia prefers moist, well-drained soil and full sun but is very adaptable to a wide variety of soil types and partial shade. Although a slow grower, it will perform admirably in many landscape situations. Amur maackia is heat, drought, cold, and pollution tolerant.

Amur maackia performs best from Zones 4–8. It is an ideal single-specimen tree near a patio or in a lawn area, and it can also be effective in groupings or raised planters. Some utility companies are planting *Maackia* as a street tree and in other urban situations.

{ *Magnolia* spp.
Magnolias

A group of about eighty species of trees and large shrubs, magnolias are primarily native to Asia and to the Americas north of the equator. There are both temperate-climate and tropical magnolias, and they can have evergreen or deciduous foliage.

As a group, magnolias are one of the most beloved flowering trees in American gardens. They are generally the first to flower in early spring, but some species are midspring and late-spring bloomers, as well. Magnolias in flower have a refreshing, lemony scent that is rivaled by few trees. The flowers range from white to yellow to deep pink, depending on the species and variety. In the North magnolia flowers are especially vulnerable to the unpredictable elements of spring, such as cold, wind, and rain. A magnolia in full bloom can easily get damaged by frost, which causes the flowers to turn brown.

After flowering finishes, lustrous green leaves unfurl. In mid- to late summer a small pinkish green, pineapplelike fruit cluster ripens, which on some species can be ornamental. Most deciduous magnolias do not offer exceptional fall foliage color, but they sometimes exhibit a yellow or yellow brown foliage at the end of the growing season. The deciduous species of magnolias have fuzzy gray flower buds that are quite interesting in the winter season.

Most magnolias prefer moist, well-drained soil and full sun or partial shade. They benefit greatly from growing in a rich, organic soil with plenty of drainage. Magnolias have very thin bark and are easily damaged

Magnolias in the spring

by lawn mowers and other power equipment, so be careful when working near these trees.

Magnolia x soulangiana (saucer magnolia)

Though there are many worthy species of magnolia. *M. x soulangiana*, saucer magnolia, and *M. stellata*, star magnolia, are two of the most popular and most widely available in the horticultural industry. Saucer magnolia is a large, coarse tree with bold, lustrous green leaves and smooth gray bark. It reaches 25–35 ft. tall, with an oval to rounded growth habit. The thick, felty flower buds expand and open to cup-shaped pink flowers that can reach 5–10 in. in diameter. As the flowers mature and the lower petals peel away, the flower looks like a

© Vincent A. Simeone

Saucer magnolia in bloom

© Vincent A. Simeone

Saucer magnolia flowers

cup sitting on a saucer. Flowers range from light pink to deep purplish pink and offer a heavenly fragrance. In full bloom this tree is magnificent.

Saucer magnolia is quite adaptable to a variety of soil types, but it thrives in moist, acidic, organic, well-drained soil. It flowers best in full sun but also performs well in partial shade. Keep it out of windy, highly exposed, or dry sites.

Because it can get quite large, a saucer magnolia should be given adequate space to spread. It is an excellent specimen tree for an open lawn area and is equally effective in small groupings. Hardy from Zones 5–9.

NOTABLE VARIETIES

'Brozzonii'. This large variety displays white flowers with accents of pale rosy pink at the base.

'Lennei'. It offers large, deep magenta-purple flowers and dark green leaves.

'Lennei Alba'. The pure white, gobletlike flowers are stunning in the spring landscape.

Magnolia stellata (star magnolia)

Typically a smaller tree than saucer magnolia, star magnolia blooms a bit earlier. It grows 15–20 ft. tall, with a slightly smaller spread. It offers pure white, star-shaped flowers with many petals. Star magnolia has a beautiful delicate appearance in spring. After the flowers finish, thin, glossy, deep green leaves develop, persisting until fall. Star magnolia also has fuzzy, gray buds and smooth, silvery gray bark.

Star magnolia is one of the most adaptable magnolias, tolerating both warm and cold climates and various soil types. It prefers moist, well-drained, rich soil and full sun but will also perform admirably in shade.

Star magnolia is a delightful small tree that is excellent for early spring color. It is an ideal specimen and can also be used in small groupings. Hardy from Zones 4–8.

NOTABLE VARIETIES

'Centennial'. A very cold-hardy and vigorous variety, it has a beautiful upright, pyramidal growth habit. The outside of the large, showy white flowers are tinged with blush pink. 'Centennial' was introduced at the Arnold Arboretum in Jamaica Plain, Massachusetts, to commemorate the garden's 100th anniversary in 1972.

'Rosea'. This beautiful variety has blush to light pink flowers.

'Royal Star'. This relatively early bloomer has a dense, shrubby growth habit to 20 ft. tall.

'Waterlily'. Truly one of the most beautiful of all of magnolia varieties, 'Waterlily' has rich pink buds, which open to white flowers with a faint pink tint on the outer edges. Tends to flower later than the species and is very fragrant.

Little Girl series

In the 1950s hybridizers at the United States National Arboretum crossed *Magnolia liliiflora* 'Nigra' with *M. stellata* 'Rosea'. The intention was to retain the showy flowering characteristics of the star magnolia but to develop later flowering to reduce the risk of frost damage. The resulting Little Girl series—including 'Ann', 'Betty', 'Jane', 'Judy', 'Pinkie', 'Randy', 'Ricki', and 'Susan'—are dwarf, relatively later-blooming magnolias that are ideal for the residential landscape. Flower

Dense, rounded habit of a Little Girl hybrid magnolia

© Vincent A. Simeone

colors range from pink to deep purple, depending on the variety. During the early summer some flowers will develop sporadically.

The Little Girl hybrids are rather shrubby, and they mature at only 10–15 ft. tall, making them ideal for the home garden. These hybrids are quite cold tolerant and amazingly versatile in the landscape. Hardy from Zones 4–7.

Yellow magnolias

In the magnolia world one of the most celebrated breakthroughs has been the development of yellow-flowering magnolias. Many of them are the results of crosses between *Magnolia denudata* (Yulan magnolia) and *M. acuminata* (cucumber magnolia). One of the first yellow magnolias that was developed and made commercially available was 'Elizabeth', introduced in 1978 by the Brooklyn Botanic Garden. To this day it is the standard by which all yellow magnolia varieties are measured. In my opinion, it is still the best yellow magnolia, taking into consideration its aesthetic value, adaptability, and vigorous growth rate. In midspring the medium to creamy yellow flowers provide a bright, showy display in the landscape. The flowers exude a sweet, lemony fragrance. 'Elizabeth' will typically bloom later than saucer magnolia and tends to be less susceptible to spring frost damage.

The growth habit of 'Elizabeth' is broadly pyramidal to 35 ft. tall. The newest introduction from the Brooklyn Botanical Garden is 'Judy Zuk', named after a great gardener and former director of the garden. It offers yellow flowers with an orangey base and a

'Elizabeth' magnolia in bloom

© Bruce Curtis

'Elizabeth' magnolia flowers up close

fruity fragrance. 'Elizabeth' has a tight, pyramidal habit while 'Judy Zuk' has a layered candelabra-like branching structure. The flowers stand out well against the lush foliage.

Other good yellow magnolia varieties include 'Butterflies' and 'Goldfinch', which offer deeper yellow flowers than 'Elizabeth'. 'Yellow Bird' has yellow flowers with a greenish color at the base while 'Yellow Lantern' offers more of a creamy yellow flower. Both cultivars also develop distinctly upright, pyramidal habits to 25 ft. in height. 'Koban Dori' is a delicate variety from Japan with soft, canary yellow flowers.

Yellow magnolias are among the most coveted flowering trees in commerce. Even nearly thirty years after their introduction, they still create excitement in the garden. Most yellow magnolias are rated for Hardiness Zones 5–9.

Magnolia macrophylla (bigleaf magnolia)

This most unusual species has giant, 1–2½ ft. long, dark green leaves with silvery undersides. The leaves have a tropical appearance and shimmer in the summer wind. In early summer large, creamy white, fragrant flowers develop on the ends of every branch. In fall a rather interesting egg-shaped, pinkish red fruit ripens and persists through most of the fall. Bigleaf magnolia makes its presence known with a dense, upright growth habit.

Bigleaf magnolia thrives in moist, organic, rich soil and full sun or partial shade. This rather peculiar tree does require space to grow and will reach 30–40 ft. tall, with a similar spread.

Bigleaf magnolia is a great tree for adding a bold, coarse texture to the landscape. It can be used as a single-specimen lawn tree or in small groupings. Hardy from Zones 5–8.

Evergreen and semi-evergreen magnolias

Several species of magnolia have evergreen or semi-evergreen leaves. Although their flower display tends not to be as profuse as those of the deciduous magnolia types, evergreen and semievergreen magnolias' unusual combination of lustrous evergreen foliage, fragrant flowers, and dense habit are quite aesthetically pleasing. The two main species are the southern magnolia (*Magnolia grandiflora*) and the sweetbay magnolia (*M. virginiana*), natives that offer unique ornamental value and exceptional landscape function.

Magnolia grandiflora (southern magnolia)

Southern magnolia, native to the southern U.S., is among the most beautiful of broad-leaved evergreens, displaying lustrous, thick, evergreen foliage and an upright, dense growth habit. Although it has long been a popular favorite in southern gardens, several new varieties of this plant will also grow in colder areas of the United States, including Zone 5.

Southern magnolia has large, shiny, dark green leaves that can reach 6 or more in. in length. Certain specimens and select varieties display a rusty brown

© Bruce Curtis

Southern magnolia foliage

coloration to the undersides of the leaves, adding a nice contrast in the landscape. The broad, pyramidal growth habit has a distinct presence. Southern magnolia flowers later than most deciduous types; the large, fragrant white flowers can reach 8–12 in. in diameter in summer. The spectacular flowers are followed by large, conelike fruit that ripen in the autumn and often persist through the winter. These interesting fruit look like small pineapples and are comprised of many small capsules, which open to expose bright red seeds.

Southern magnolia is a remarkably resilient tree, tolerating poor soil, including heavy clay and sandy loam. It prefers moist, rich, well-drained, acidic soil, and full sun or partial shade. In northern climates southern magnolia can be planted in full sun or partial shade but should be sheltered from wind.

Especially in warmer climates southern magnolia can develop into a large tree and must be given ample room to grow. Mature specimens can reach 60 or more ft. in the South, although they remain much smaller in colder climates. Typically, I have seen specimens in northern gardens growing up to 40 ft. tall.

Southern magnolia can be used as a single specimen or in groupings. It is also a shade-tolerant tree and can be effectively used as a tall screening plant. Southern magnolia will make a bold statement and significant visual impact in the landscape. Hardy from Zones 6–9, but several varieties have shown hardiness to Zone 5.

NOTABLE VARIETIES

'Brackens Brown Beauty'. This excellent selection has deep green, glossy foliage above and a rusty brown color on the underside. It has also shown reliable cold hardiness.

'D.D. Blanchard'. A beautiful tree with a distinct pyramidal growth habit and dark green foliage with rusty brown undersides.

'Edith Bogue'. One of the most popular and cold-hardy varieties of southern magnolia, it features large, dark green leaves and large white flowers.

'Little Gem'. This dwarf variety—with small, dark green leaves and a tight, pyramidal growth habit to 20 ft. high—is ideal for the landscape with limited space.

Magnolia virginiana (sweetbay magnolia)

Sweetbay magnolia has 3–5 in. long, dark green leaves with silvery white undersides. In even the slightest of breezes, the leaves shimmer as they flutter. In northern climates this tree tends to be semievergreen to nearly deciduous, depending on the severity of the winter. In warmer, southern climates it will usually retain its lustrous, evergreen foliage. The leaves and twigs offer a spicy fragrance when bruised. In colder climates this small native tree will grow up to 20 ft. tall and have a narrow habit, but in southern gardens it can grow much larger.

Sweetbay magnolia displays creamy white flowers in late spring and early summer. Often this tree will sporadically bloom into late summer. The small flowers have a sweet fragrance. In addition, sweetbay magnolia has smooth, silvery gray bark and a small but interesting fruit cluster. The plants can be trained as a multistemmed large shrub or as a single-stem small tree.

Sweetbay magnolia prefers full sun or partial shade and moist, well-drained soil but is very adaptable. It will also grow in wet soil near streams and ponds.

Sweetbay magnolia is excellent as a single specimen or in small groupings. It can be used in native, woodland settings or in a cultivated landscape near a patio or deck or in a lawn area. Hardy from Zones 5–9. This tree can be found growing all along the East Coast and as far west as Texas.

NOTABLE VARIETIES

'Henry Hicks' and 'Milton'. These two superior varieties with dark, evergreen leaves are supposedly more reliably evergreen than the species.

Other magnolia species, cultivars, and hybrids

Many excellent magnolia hybrids have been developed to offer exceptionally ornamental flowers in a wide variety of colors, ranging from deep reddish pink to purple and even to yellow. The 'Wadas Memory', 'Galaxy', 'Spectrum', and Loebner magnolias are a few especially good hybrids that are suitable for the home landscape.

Magnolia kobus 'Wadas Memory' is a beautiful flowering tree with a neat, extraordinarily dense, strongly pyramidal growth habit and large, frilly white flowers. After flowering has finished, the new foliage emerges a beautiful bronze, before maturing to dark, glossy green. Even in summer this tree is very interesting, with its tight, conical growth habit.

'Wadas Memory' is an excellent specimen tree in a lawn area—especially for a limited space—because it gets much taller than it spreads. Although somewhat

© Vincent A. Simeone

'Wadas Memory' magnolia in bloom

difficult to find in nurseries, it is well worth the hunt. Hardy from Zones 5–8.

Magnolia x 'Galaxy' is one of my favorite varieties of magnolia for the residential landscape. 'Galaxy' offers an upright, pyramidal growth habit when young, and a rounded canopy as it ages. The deep reddish purple flowers provide a rich, vibrant color in the spring land-

Deep reddish pink flowers and pyramidal habit of 'Galaxy'

'Spectrum' is very closely related to 'Galaxy' and shares many of its ornamental features. 'Spectrum' does offer slightly larger flowers and a broader growth habit than does 'Galaxy'. Both varieties are quite adaptable to various soil types and light levels but thrive in moist, organic, well-drained soil and full sun or partial shade. Because of their pyramidal growth habits, these two varieties are useful in residential landscapes. They are ideal in a lawn area, near a patio, or in combination with other flowering shrubs and trees. Hardy from Zones 5–8, and possibly 9 with specific siting.

Magnolia x *loebneri* (Loebner magnolia) is a wonderful hybrid magnolia with several exceptional varieties that make great additions to the spring landscape. Loebner magnolia, a cross between star magnolia and kobus magnolia, has noticeable traits from each parent. This medium-sized tree has showy, pure white flowers in early spring and dark green summer foliage. The growth habit is upright and broad to rounded over time.

NOTABLE VARIETIES

Here are a few excellent varieties of Loebner magnolias worthy of inclusion in the garden.

'Ballerina'. The beautiful pure white flowers have pinkish centers. It grows to 25 ft. tall.

'Leonard Messel'. This small tree to 20 ft. tall is truly one of my favorite deciduous magnolia varieties. It displays showy light purplish pink, star-shaped flowers in early spring.

'Merrill', sometimes seen in the nursery trade as 'Dr. Merrill'. A large-flowering form, it has flowers 3½ in. in diameter.

scape. As the flowers open, they expose their lighter pink interior, which offers a nice contrast to the dark outer portions. This small tree can reach 20–30 ft. tall, with a slightly less spread.

© Vincent A. Simeone

'Leonard Messel' magnolia in bloom

{ *Malus* spp.
Crabapple

Crabapples are unquestionably some of the most diverse and versatile of all flowering trees, especially in the northeastern and midwestern United States. Approximately thirty-five species and over eight hundred garden varieties of crabapples blanket landscapes all across the globe. Crabapples offer showy, single or double white, pink, or reddish purple flowers in spring and small fruit that look like miniature apples. The fruit can range in color from golden yellow to deep ruby red and typically develops in the summer and fall months. Though typically very tart, the fruit may be eaten by birds and other small animals.

Flowering crabapples are notoriously susceptible to several leaf and stem diseases, such as leaf spot, apple scab, rust, and fire blight. However, today there are many new and improved varieties that show remarkable resistance to these problems. Crabapples are incredibly adaptable trees, tolerating heat, drought, cold, pollution, various soil types and pH levels, and a range of light exposure levels. For best results, though, crabapples should be placed in full sun and moist, well-drained soil.

More so than other flowering trees, crabapple can be fairly high maintenance when it comes to pruning. Typically, crabapples develop watersprouts and suckers, which are vegetative shoots that grow from the branches and roots of the tree. This vegetative growth will produce leaves but no flowers, and if too much of this growth forms, it may reduce flowering on your tree. Therefore, an ongoing pruning program is needed to reduce the amount of suckers and watersprouts that develop. If you have an older tree with a large amount of suckering or watersprouts, some thinning can be done, but do not remove all of this growth in one season. Instead, early every summer remove just a percentage of the unwanted growth after the tree has finished flowering, gradually, over several years, pruning all of it away. For example, remove a third of the suckers or watersprout growth each year and spread this selective pruning over three years.

Crabapples are used in numerous landscape situations—as single specimens, in groupings, in planters, espaliered, and for many more functions. They can be used in commercial settings or in the home landscape;

Crabapples in the landscape

they are often found in parks, in urban conditions, and even near the seashore. Most crabapple types have a hardiness range from Zones 4–8.

Several species and newer varieties offer exceptional beauty and function in the landscape. *Malus floribunda* (Japanese flowering crabapple) is an old-fashioned species with pink flower buds opening to white flowers. It also offers yellow to red fruit and a broad to rounded growth habit to 25 ft. tall.

Malus sargentii (Sargent crabapple) is a shrubby form with a low, spreading, mounded habit to 10 ft. tall. Red flower buds open to white flowers and eventually develop bright red fruit. Sargent crabapple is excellent for raised planters and in areas with limited space.

Malus sieboldii var. *zumi* 'Calocarpa' (Zumi crabapple), an old favorite, has red flower buds and pure white flowers. The bright red fruit is densely clustered. This species will develop a dense, rounded habit to 25 ft. tall.

NOTABLE VARIETIES

Many new varieties offer improved disease resistance and ornamental value. In addition, many hold onto their fruit well into the fall and winter and are not considered messy.

'Adams'. This tree grows 20–25 ft. tall and offers rosy pink flowers, followed by small red fruit.

'Callaway'. This is one of the favorite white-flowered crabapples for gardens in the southeastern United States. It features pink buds that open to showy white flowers. This is also one of the largest-fruiting types, with red apples reaching 1 in. in diameter; when ripe they are one of the sweetest tasting crabapples available.

'Centurion'. This variety grows 25 ft. tall and 15–20 ft. wide. The red buds open to rose red flowers, and the fruit is a bright, glossy red color.

'Donald Wyman'. Named after the great horticulturist from Arnold Arboretum, this tree displays red flower buds changing to pink and opening to white flowers. Fruit is bright glossy red. Excellent disease resistance and reliability.

'Harvest Gold'. This variety offers pink buds opening to white flowers, followed by unusual glossy, golden yellow fruit that persists until early winter.

'Indian Magic'. This tree grows 15–20 ft. tall, with a similar spread. The red flower buds open to dark pink flowers. The delicate fruit ranges from red to orange.

'Indian Summer'. This crabapple grows to 20 ft. tall. It displays rose red flowers and small, bright red fruit.

'Molten Lava'. A weeping growth habit distinguishes this tree, which grows 15 ft. tall and 12 ft. wide. The deep red buds open to white flowers; the small fruit is reddish orange.

'Prairifire'. This tree grows 20 ft. tall, with a similar spread. The showy, dark pinkish red blooms give way to small, reddish purple fruit.

Red Jewel ('Jewelcole'). This outstanding variety has beautiful white flowers and glossy, bright red fruit that will persist well into the winter months.

'Snowdrift'. This small tree has a dense, rounded habit to 15 ft. tall. The profuse white flowers and orange-red fruits are both exceptional qualities. In addition, the summer foliage is a lustrous dark green.

'Strawberry Parfait'. Showy, long-lasting pink flowers are rimmed with a darker pink margin, providing the blooms a two-tone effect. New foliage emerges reddish purple in the spring and matures to a rich, deep green in the summer. Deep red fruit persists late into the fall. The growth habit is irregular and spreading, reaching a height of about 20 ft., with a slightly larger spread.

Sugar Tyme ('Sutgzam'). This is my favorite variety of crabapple because of its floral display, long-lasting fruit, and disease resistance. 'Sugar Tyme' has pink flower buds, opening to pure, sugar white flowers, and large, glossy, deep red fruit, which often persists into midwinter. A real knockout!

© Vincent A. Simeone

Sugar Tyme crabapple in flower

© Bruce Curtis

Glossy, red fruit of Sugar Tyme crabapple

{ *Oxydendrum arboreum*
Sourwood

Sourwood, sometimes known as the sorrell tree, is native to the southeastern United States and up to Pennsylvania. It is one of the most ornamental native flowering trees available to the gardener who is willing to take the time to enjoy its unique beauty. Sourwood is a four-season tree, offering flowers, summer and fall foliage interest, and even ornamental value in the winter landscape. Its flowers attract bees and butterflies into the garden.

Sourwood displays lush, glossy, dark green leaves during the summer and fragrant flowers that look like lily of the valley flowers as they hang in long clusters. As fall approaches, golden yellow fruit clusters form, offering a wonderful contrast to the deep reddish maroon fall foliage. The fruit clusters resemble golden tassels against the foliage. Sourwood's combination of fruit and foliage in the fall is one of the most eye-catching sights of any landscape tree. In the winter the brown seedpods persist, and on mature trees rough, deeply fissured bark develops.

Sourwood is related to rhododendrons and azaleas and prefers similar growing conditions. It thrives in moist, organic, acidic, rich soil and partial shade. It will also grow well in full sun, as long as adequate moisture is provided. Gardeners must be patient with this lovely tree because it is a slow grower. Like all things that are worth the wait, sourwood will not disappoint.

Sourwood has a strongly pyramidal growth habit and will eventually grow 20–30 ft. tall. It is an excellent small specimen tree for a woodland garden or as a single-specimen lawn tree. It is also effective in small groupings. Sourwood mixes wonderfully with rhododendrons, holly, dogwoods, and other acid-loving plants. Hardy from Zones 5–9.

© Bruce Curtis

Deep red fall foliage and golden yellow fruit clusters of sourwood

{ *Parrotia persica*
Persian parrotia

Persian parrotia is one of the most beautiful medium-sized trees because it offers unique ornamental qualities all four seasons. Though this relative of witch hazel is native to Iran, it will perform well in colder northern climates. *Parrotia* can be grown as a single-stem or multistemmed tree. It has lustrous, dark green foliage that turns brilliant shades of red, maroon, orange, and yellow in the fall—sometimes all four colors at one time. *Parrotia* also has delicate, frilly, deep maroon flowers that open in late winter. But the most striking ornamental qualities of this exotic plant come with its bark, which is exfoliating and multicolored, displaying brown, gray, cream, and green. This bark interest along with *Parrotia's* irregular branching habit set it apart from the rest. These ornamental characteristics are most noticeable in the stark winter landscape.

Parrotia should be grown in moist, well-drained soil and full sun or partial shade. It adapts well to various soil types and environmental conditions, including clay soil, heat, humidity, drought, and cold. Parrotia tends to be fast growing during its youth and slower growing as it matures; it can grow to 20–30 ft. high and wide. As *Parrotia* matures, it develops twisted, sinuous branching pattern and an upright, spreading growth habit. 'Vanessa' is a variety that offers a distinctly upright, columnar growth habit.

Parrotia is a medium- to fast-growing tree that can be effective as a single-specimen tree in a garden or lawn area. It can easily function as a focal point in the landscape. This tree is hardy from Zones 4–8.

Persian parrotia is one of the most unusual exotic trees for the landscape.

{ *Photinia* spp.
Photinia
Photinia villosa (Oriental photinia)

Oriental photinia can be grown as a large, multi-stemmed shrub or a small, single-stemmed tree. It can reach 10–15 ft. tall, with slightly less of a spread. Oriental photinia is very adaptable and offers several seasons of interest. In spring small clusters of white flowers open, contrasting well against the rich, dark green leaves. This plant often glows with color in the fall landscape, the foliage turning brilliant shades of orangey yellow and red. Also in the fall, small, bright red fruit ripen and will persist until early winter.

As mentioned, Oriental photinia can be trained as a single-stem or multistemmed small tree. This is

© Bruce Curtis

White flower clusters of Oriental photinia

© Vincent A. Simeone

Golden yellow fall foliage of Oriental photinia

accomplished by selecting one or several strong stems and removing all other stems. As the tree matures, the lower branches can be removed to encourage a tree-like habit.

Oriental photinia prefers moist, well-drained soil but is remarkably adaptable to many soil types, drought, and heat. It thrives in full sun but will also perform well in partial shade. Pruning at a young age is recommended to train and shape your plant.

Oriental photinia can be used in small groupings or as a single specimen. It works well with other flowering trees or shrubs or as a stand-alone tree. It even works well near the seashore and in urban conditions. Hardy from Zones 4–7.

Photinia serrulata (Chinese photinia)

In addition to the deciduous Oriental photinia, there are several evergreen species of *Photinia*. Chinese photinia (*P. serrulata*) is a broadleaf evergreen that will grow 30 ft. or more tall, with dense growth. The dark green, lustrous, finely serrated leaves are thick and leathery. The new growth is tinged with a pink coloration, but as the leaves mature, they change to deep green. The white flower clusters offer a showy display in spring, as well. After the flowers fade, bright red fruit forms; it will persist into the winter months. Although not commonly found in commerce and underutilized, this evergreen is far superior to the common red-tip photinia (*Photinia* x *fraseri*), which is so prevalent in landscapes across the southeastern United States. Chinese photinia prefers moist, well-drained soil but tolerates a wide range of soils and is quite drought tolerant, once established. It will perform well in full sun or partial shade. Chinese photinia can be used in a grouping as a tall screen or as a single-specimen evergreen tree. Hardy from Zones 7–9.

Prunus spp.
Ornamental cherry, plum, and apricot

Although many species of cherry are appreciated for their edible fruit, numerous cherries are also grown for their ornamental characteristics: showy spring flowers, ornamental foliage, and beautifully textured bark. The *Prunus* genus includes many different types of flowering trees—notably, cherries, plums, and apricots grown for their ornamental characteristics and not their fruit. *Prunus* offers a wide range of flower colors, from white to deep rosy pink. The foliage can range from rich green to reddish maroon, depending on the species and variety in question.

Cherries can also offer quite a diverse selection of bark colors and textures, which are most noticeable in the winter months. Cherry bark has *lenticels*, which are small glands arranged in an irregular pattern. The lenticels and the variations of smooth- and rough-textured bark of the stems make *Prunus* quite interesting most of the year. Bark color on ornamental *Prunus* can range from tan to gray-brown to dark brown, depending on the species.

In general, flowering cherries, apricots, and plums perform best in moist, well-drained, acidic soil and full

© Vincent A. Simeone

Horizontal lenticels on cherry bark

sun or partial shade. They are quite adaptable and drought tolerant once established. They are susceptible to various insects and diseases, so careful monitoring is essential to ensure that your trees remain healthy.

The siting of these ornamental trees is important, in order for you to be able to enjoy their interesting color and texture fully. *Prunus* species are very effective when used as single specimens, in small groupings, or in larger mass plantings. The mass plantings of ornamental cherries in Washington, D.C., are a breathtaking sight to behold early in the spring, when the city

Yoshino cherry in flower

hosts an annual cherry blossom festival, which attracts thousands of visitors. The festival is the result of a gift of three thousand cherry trees from the city of Tokyo to Washinton, D.C., in 1912.

Many species and varieties of *Prunus* can be used in the residential landscape. Three of the most commonly available cherries are Oriental cherry (*P. serrulata*), weeping Higan cherry (*P. subhirtella* 'Pendula'), and Yoshino cherry (*P.* × *yedoensis*).

Prunus serrulata (Oriental flowering cherry)

Oriental flowering cherry is an old-fashioned cherry that is still one of the most popular in American gardening. It is highly cultivated and offers the greatest selection of flower types and colors of any cherry. This species, *Prunus serrulata*, can get big and gawky if sited in a small landscape with limited room, so careful attention should be paid to selecting the right location. Most *P. serrulata* varieties will grow 20–35 ft. tall and wide. The flowers can range from single to double and from white to deep pink, depending on the variety chosen. The new foliage can range from bright green to bronze, but when mature it changes to a rich green. Fall foliage colors range from bronze and orange to deep red.

Oriental cherry can be effective as a single-specimen lawn tree or in small groupings. It is hardy from Zones 5–8.

NOTABLE VARIETIES

'Amanogawa'. An interesting variety with a very narrow, upright growth habit, it features fragrant pink flowers in spring. Mature specimens can reach 20 ft. tall, but with only a 5 ft. spread, making 'Amanogawa' excellent where space is limited.

'Kwanzan'. This is easily the most popular variety of this species. The double flowers are a deep pink, and they stay this way for a week or two before fading to a paler pink. I do not prefer this variety—because the flower color is almost too bright. Several other varieties listed are a bit more pleasing to the eye.

'Mount Fuji' ('Shirotae'). A rather handsome small tree with a spreading habit, this variety has pink flower buds opening to pure white flowers.

'Shirofugen'. This beautiful variety features deep pink buds, opening to double flowers that are blush pink to pure white. As the flowers age, they turn deeper pink before falling. The new foliage, a deep bronze color, offers a wonderful accent to the showy blooms.

Prunus subhirtella 'Pendula' (weeping Higan cherry)

This popular spring bloomer has a graceful weeping habit and small, single pink flowers in early spring. Flower color can range from pale to deep pink. After flowering has finished, long, lustrous green leaves emerge and turn shades of yellow or reddish maroon

© Vincent A. Simeone

Pink flowers and bronze foliage of 'Shirofugen' cherry

© Vincent A. Simeone

Delicate pink flowers of Higan cherry

Weeping Higan cherry in flower

in the fall. The bark of weeping Higan cherry ranges from brown to light tan or gray.

Weeping Higan cherry is very effective as a single specimen or in groupings. It is truly a four-season treasure because of its flowers, foliage, and graceful habit. This cherry is hardy from Zones 4–8, but it will grow in Zone 9 with proper siting in a cool, moist area of the garden.

In addition to the weeping Higan cherry, 'Autumnalis' is an excellent *P. subhirtella* variety worthy of landscape use. It has a upright, spreading habit and will flower both in the spring and in the fall. The flowers are pinkish white and semi-double. The spring display tends to be profuse, whereas the fall display of flowers is rather sporadic. 'Autumnalis' is a very charming small tree for spring, summer, and fall interest. 'Autumnalis Rosea' offers deeper pink flowers.

Prunus x *yedoensis* (Yoshino cherry)

The Yoshino cherry is a hybrid that was first introduced in Tokyo in 1872 and is now one of the most popular cultivated flowering cherries. Yoshino cherry is a lovely flowering tree, with masses of small, single white flowers in early spring. The delicate petals look like falling snow as they drift to the ground. Although all too short lived, this most magnificent floral display will undoubtedly leave an indelible impression on those who behold it. After the flowers finish, dark green leaves emerge and in the autumn they will turn yellow or orange, sometimes accented with deep shades of reddish maroon. The lightly colored, gray-tan bark is very noticeable in winter.

Yoshino cherry is very adaptable but performs best in full sun. It has a wide-spreading, rounded growth habit usually reaching 25–35 ft. tall and wide. It can be used as a single-specimen lawn tree or near a patio. It is often found in large sites, such as parks and public gardens in groupings. Many specimens of Yoshino cherry sprinkle the landscape in our nation's capital. Hardy from Zones 5–8.

NOTABLE VARIETIES

'Afterglow'. This very attractive variety has deep pink flowers that positively glow in the landscape.

'Akebono'. This tree is similar to 'Afterglow', but its flowers are a softer pink color. It has a spreading growth habit.

© Vincent A. Simeone

'Akebono' cherry blossoms

'Shidare Yoshino'. This weeping Yoshino cherry features white blossoms and a graceful cascading growth habit.

'Snow Fountains'. A semiweeping form, it offers showy white flowers and a mounded growth habit reaching 6–12 ft. tall, with a similar spread. Excellent for gardens with limited space.

Prunus x *incam* 'Okame' ('Okame' cherry)

This upright, medium-sized cherry offers delicate, single, rosy pink flowers in early spring around the same time the magnolias bloom. 'Okame' also has small, dark green leaves that turn deep orange or bronzy red during the autumn. The upright, vase-shaped growth habit and smooth, reddish brown bark accented with gray lenticels offer interest even when the plant is not in bloom or in leaf. Overall, this tree provides delicate, fine texture and pleasing ornamental qualities that span all four seasons.

'Okame' cherry grows 20–30 ft. high, with a smaller spread, and is hardy from Zones 6–8. It is ideal as a single specimen or in small groupings in areas of the garden where winter interest and early spring color is desired. 'Okame' makes a very useful tree for casting light shade onto a patio or in a lawn area. This tree is also being used as a street tree and in public parks because it is tough and adaptable.

'Okame' cherry in the landscape

© Vincent A. Simeone

Prunus x 'Hally Jolivette' ('Hally Jolivette' cherry)

The 'Hally Jolivette' cherry is a small flowering cherry that is very suitable for the garden with limited space. Fine-textured, it can be trained as a single-stemmed tree or a multistemmed large shrub. The flowers emerge in spring—light pink or nearly white, often with deep pink centers—and last for several weeks. This delicate tree is breathtaking in flower. The small, glossy green leaves will change to shades of bronze, orange, red, and maroon in the fall. Once the leaves drop in the autumn, the light, grayish tan stems and branches with noticeable lenticels are uncovered. The stems are very slender, so even in winter this tree offers an interesting, fine texture.

Delicate, pink flowers of 'Hally Jolivette' cherry

© Bruce Curtis

© Vincent A. Simeone

A grouping of 'Hally Jolivette' cherries

'Hally Jolivette' cherry prefers full sun or partial shade and moist, well-drained soil, but it is very adaptable. Pruning can be kept to a minimum because this tree will not grow very large, but occasional selective pruning may be desired to keep plants tidy. Some training at a young age will prove beneficial in establishing a strong, healthy tree.

This variety of cherry is without question one of my most favorite of all flowering cherry trees. In the formal gardens at Planting Fields Arboretum, Oyster Bay, New York, we have strategically placed several 'Hally Jolivette' specimens in the landscape. I can walk past these trees in bloom a hundred times during the spring and never grow tired of their unbridled beauty.

'Hally Jolivette' cherry will reach 15 ft. tall, with a similar spread, and is hardy from Zones 5–7.

Prunus mume (Japanese apricot)

Japanese apricot is a handsome ornamental flowering tree that reaches 20 ft. tall, with a dense, rounded growth habit. The fragrant flowers can be single or double and range in color from red to pink or white. The floral display is quite showy: the shiny green stems contrast well with the individual, rounded flowers. Flowering can start as early as midwinter, continuing through early spring. In addition to the beautiful flowers, flowering apricot offers dark brown bark with noticeable lenticels and lustrous, dark green leaves in the summer. Often

A young Japanese apricot in bloom

Bright pink flowers of Japanese apricot

overlooked is the small but interesting yellow fruit, which is not considered edible in American gardens, although in Asia it is a delicacy prepared several ways.

This delightful, small, fast-growing, flowering tree is a favorite in Japan. The popularity of this plant in American gardens was the result of the tireless efforts of the late J. C. Raulston, a famed horticulturist at North Carolina State University. Today more and more gardeners are learning about the great virtues this small flowering tree has to offer.

Like most other *Prunus*, Japanese apricot prefers moist, well-drained soil and full sun or partial shade. It can be used in small groupings or as a single specimen tree in a lawn. It is hardy from Zones 6–9.

NOTABLE VARIETIES

'Bonita'. Rose red, semidouble flowers offer a nice contrast to the deep olive green stems of this very vigorous, easy-to-grow plant.

'Matsubara Red'. This apricot has not only dark red, double flowers but new growth also has a reddish hue, which will turn green with age.

'Peggy Clarke'. This popular variety has double rose pink flowers with long stamens and red calyces.

'Rosemary Clarke'. This variety offers double white flowers; it is somewhat difficult to find in the nursery trade.

'W. B. Clarke'. An apricot with double pink flowers and a weeping habit.

Purple-leaved *Prunus* types

Although many species offer lustrous, dark green

foliage, there are also several types with deep reddish maroon summer foliage. Blireana plum (*Prunus* x *blireana*) has double pink flowers and reddish purple foliage in early spring, which fades to green in the summer. This interesting tree grows to 20 ft. tall and is hardy from Zones 5–8.

Another common *Prunus* with purple foliage is the 'Schubert' chokecherry, *Prunus virginiana* 'Schubert'. This vigorous grower can reach 20–35 ft. tall and displays showy clusters of white flowers in spring. The new growth is green, and the mature foliage is deep purple. The fruit of chokecherry is used to produce jams, jellies, pies, and wines. This cherry is suited only to the cooler, northern climates of North America and is hardy from Zones 2–5, but it will also adapt to Zone 6 and the northern part of Zone 7.

Prunus x *cistena*, purpleleaf sand cherry, is very similar to *P. cerasifera* 'Atropurpurea' (described below) because *P. cerasifera* is one of its parents. The sand cherry's foliage is more ruby purple to reddish purple, though, and it has a smaller, shrubby habit to 10 ft. tall. Single, pink flowers open after the leaves have emerged in spring, and the two offer a nice contrast. This extremely tough, adaptable tree thrives in hot, dry conditions and sandy soil. It will also perform well in well-drained, rich garden soil. Purpleleaf sand cherry is best in full sun, but partial shade is also acceptable. It is excellent in the landscape with limited space. Hardy from Zones 2–8.

Probably the most common of all of the purpleleafed *Prunus* is purpleleaf, or Pissard, plum, *Prunus*

cerasifera 'Atropurpurea'. This small-flowering tree has an upright, broad habit to 25 ft. tall. Generally, the small pink flowers arrive before the deep reddish purple leaves in spring but sometimes occur simultaneously. Even though the flowers are small, the floral display is quite effective. The foliage will remain purple the entire summer and into the fall, until they drop with the onset of cold weather.

Purpleleaf plum prefers moist, well-drained soil and full sun. It will tolerate partial shade, as well, but do not put it in too much shade. It's quite adaptable to various soil types and pH levels, even heavy clay soils.

Purpleleaf plum can be used as a single specimen or in groupings. Its foliage makes it an excellent accent plant in a lawn area or in a summer landscape that offers a primarily green backdrop. This *Prunus* is hardy from Zones 5–8, but it may grow in Zone 4 with protection.

NOTABLE VARIETIES

These are other attractive *Prunus cerasifera* varieties.

'Krauter Vesuvius'. The dark reddish purple foliage and light pink flowers are quite interesting. This variety is similar to 'Thundercloud', but the flowers arrive earlier and are a lighter pink.

'Newport'. New foliage emerges a bronze purple color, maturing to deep reddish purple. The profusion of flowers in spring is pale pink to nearly white.

'Thundercloud'. This is probably the most popular variety of purpleleaf plum. 'Thundercloud' holds its deep purple foliage color all summer. The small, delicate pink flowers are fragrant.

'Thundercloud' plum in the landscape

© Vincent A. Simeone

'Thundercloud' plum flowers up close

{ *Ptelea trifoliata*
Hoptree

A rather unusual native tree, hoptree has dark green, trifoliate leaves in spring and summer and showy yellow fall color. In early summer small, greenish white, star-shaped flowers form, and although they are not showy, they do offer a potent fragrance. Dense clusters of winged green fruit form, turning brown as they mature. Often the interesting fruit will persist until early winter. Hoptree, also known as water ash, prefers moist, well-drained soil and full sun or partial shade. It will perform remarkably well in a partially or even densely shaded area of the garden. It typically forms a rounded, shrubby habit to 15 or 20 ft. tall.

Hoptree is an excellent woodland or understory tree and can also be used as a single specimen or in small groupings. Although somewhat hard to find commercially, its versatility and durability in the landscape make it well worth the effort. Hardy from Zones 3–9.

{ *Pterostyrax hispidus*
Epaulette tree

This rather unique, handsome tree offers several seasons of interest in the landscape. After the large, medium-green leaves unfold, 5–10 in. long, dangling white flower clusters hang like chains off the branches in early summer. The flowers have a subtle fragrance and last several weeks, before changing into fuzzy, brown fruit clusters. The flowers hang from one side and resemble the epaulettes (ornamental shoulder pieces) found on some military uniforms; thus, the common name. The unusual fruit persist until fall. The habit of this Japanese native is upright and rounded, reaching 30 ft. tall.

Epaulette tree deserves much more credit as an ornamental tree for the home garden than it receives. It is quite adaptable but thrives in full sun or partial shade and moist, acidic, well-drained soil. Winter pruning to remove dead branches or to train young trees is recommended. Epaulette tree thrives in hot, dry sunny locations.

Epaulette tree has great potential as a specimen lawn tree for the residential landscape. It is also very effective in small groupings. It's hardy from Zones 4–8, but it is better suited to colder climates.

© Bruce Curtis

Long, dangling flowers of epaulette tree

© Bruce Curtis

Epaulette tree fruit clusters

{ *Pyrus* spp.
Pear

Pyrus calleryana (Callery pear)

Like ornamental cherry, plum, and crabapple, this species of flowering tree is grown only for its ornamental attributes, not for edible fruit. Though most horticulturists and landscape professionals consider 'Bradford' pear—the most common variety of Callery pear—a weedy, poorly structured tree, there are several other important varieties that do have redeeming qualities.

Callery pear, a medium-sized tree, has an upright, pyramidal growth habit in youth, becoming upright oval or broad oval and spreading with maturity. The showy white flower clusters are typically 2–3 in. across, but they do not offer a pleasant fragrance. The rich, glossy, green, luxuriant foliage emerges after the flowers and changes to yellow, orange, scarlet, and reddish maroon in the fall. Often this species holds onto its foliage late into the fall season. The bark of Callery pear is gray, and as the tree matures, the main trunk becomes fissured.

Callery pear is not very picky when it comes to the environment it grows in. It will tolerate poor, dry soil; heavy, clay soil; and varying soil pH. Ideally, it thrives in moist, well-drained soil and full sun or partial shade, but it's very versatile. It is extremely tolerant of soil compaction, pollution, heat, and drought, which is why so many Callery pears have been planted as street trees and in other urban landscapes. Certain varieties are more susceptible than others to fire blight, a devastating disease that can kill large sections of the canopy. Small,

inconspicuous, brown fruit will form after the tree flowers. Seedlings will litter the landscape, and it is considered invasive in some parts of the U.S. Most varieties of Callery pear grow 20–40 ft. tall and are hardy from Zones 5–8, and possibly 9 with specific siting.

Callery pear's horticultural value and landscape function largely depend on the specific variety that is selected. By far the most common variety—the one that has been mass-produced and mass-planted over the years—is 'Bradford', which is not a good street tree or garden specimen, due to its vulnerability to breakage. Because of its poor growth structure, wind, ice, and other environmental conditions can cause large stems or branches to break apart from the main trunk. 'Bradford' becomes a liability as it matures, and it is virtually useless as it slowly (or if you are lucky, quickly) breaks apart. Because of this problem, 'Bradford' is considered a somewhat disposable tree in the landscape. Unfortunately, 'Bradford' was, until recently, one of the most widely distributed of any flowering tree.

One bad pear doesn't spoil the whole bunch, though. There are several garden varieties of *Pyrus calleryana* that make excellent specimens, lawn trees, urban trees, and even street trees. Their ornamental attributes and improved branching structures make them worthy of selection.

NOTABLE VARIETIES

'Aristocrat'. This variety has a pyramidal growth habit and an attractive wavy leaf margin. Its flowering is sometimes not as profuse as that of 'Bradford', but it's still very attractive. 'Aristocrat' also offers excellent reddish orange in the fall. There have been some reports of susceptibility to fire blight in southern states.

'Capital'. A variety best suited to northern gardens because of its susceptibility to fire blight, it has a distinctly columnar growth habit and lustrous, dark green leaves.

'Cleveland Select', also known as 'Chanticleer', 'Select', or 'Stone Hill'. This variety is becoming increasingly popular. It offers profuse flowering and a reddish purple fall color. The strong upright, pyramidal habit is resistant to breakage in the landscape.

'Redspire'. This variety offers a narrow, pyramidal habit and good yellow, orange, to red fall foliage. Like 'Capital', it is a variety best suited to northern gardens, where fire blight is not as much of an issue as in the South.

© Bruce Curtis

Callery pear flowers

© Bruce Curtis

'Redspire' Callery pear in full bloom

Pyrus salicifolia (willowleaf pear)

Many fruit trees are grown for their flowers and not their fruit, but few flowering fruit trees are grown for their foliage and not their flowers. *Pyrus salicifolia*, willowleaf pear, is such a species, and it is gaining in popularity in American gardens. This unusual tree is mainly grown for its dense habit and its exquisite narrow, woolly gray foliage. Long and thin like a willow's, this pear's leaves have silvery white undersides that glisten in the summer sun.

Willowleaf pear will grow 15–25 ft. tall and is hardy from Zones 4–7. I have seen this species used very effectively as a single specimen, in a grouping, or trained along a wall or fence as an espalier. 'Pendula' is a weeping variety with graceful drooping branches.

Rhus spp.
Sumacs
Rhus chinensis (Chinese sumac)

This small tree is interesting in leaf and in flower and is especially valuable late in the growing season. Chinese sumac is a large, spreading shrub or small tree to 25 ft. tall, with a similar spread. It has lush, bright green, pinnately compound leaves made up of many leaflets. The leaves turn shades of yellow, orange, or red, offering an attractive fall display. Fleecy 5–10 in. long spikes of white flowers form in late summer and persist for several weeks.

Like all sumacs, this tree prefers a hot, dry, well-drained location and full sun, although it is adaptable to various soils and levels of light exposure. Chinese sumac is ideal in barren, rocky soil

and near the seashore. It is heat, drought, and pollution tolerant.

Chinese sumac is a very effective specimen tree in a lawn area. It is also valuable in urban settings where harsh environmental conditions are prevalent. It is hardy from Zones 5–7, but it will also grow fairly well in Zone 8.

NOTABLE VARIETY

'September Beauty'. This was selected by the great Dr. Elwin Orton of Rutgers University, New Jersey, for its larger flowers and tree-type habit. It also offers a beautiful apricot-yellow foliage color in fall.

Native sumacs

Several other species of sumacs will leave a lasting impression during the late summer and fall seasons, but a couple of natives are especially noteworthy. Both smooth sumac, *Rhus glabra*, and staghorn sumac, *R. typhina*, can be grown as large, spreading shrubs or small trees. Both are somewhat irregular in their growth habits and often form dense colonies. These sumacs have long, deep green, compound leaves that turn brilliant shades of orange or red in the fall. The fall color will light up the landscape for several weeks.

Both smooth and staghorn sumac are dioecious, meaning the male and female flowers are on separate plants. The female plants offer noticeable cone-shaped, yellowish green flower spikes in midsummer, which turn deep red in late summer and fall. The fruit will persist into late winter, providing a high-protein food source for migratory birds. In winter the bare, gnarled, irregular stems and cone-shaped fruit are quite a sight to behold. The most distinct difference between these two species is in the texture of the stems. Smooth sumac has smooth stems, whereas staghorn sumac stems have noticeable thick hairs that provide a felty texture.

These sumacs thrive in hot, dry, sunny locations, like Chinese sumac, and are often found along highways and in natural areas growing in sandy, rocky soil. Staghorn sumac is often found in the cultivated garden setting, whereas smooth sumac is generally found in the wild. Both species can be trained as small trees and can be used as single specimens or in groupings. Smooth sumac ranges from 10–15 ft. tall, and staghorn sumac can reach 15–25 ft. Each species has a 'Laciniata' garden variety that offers finely cut, ferny leaves. *R. glabra* is hardy from Zones 3–9, and *R. typhina* is hardy from Zones 4–8.

Robinia pseudoacacia
Black locust

Black locust, although native to some parts of the United States, is generally considered an invasive species because of its ability to grow in barren, infertile soil and any level of light exposure. Certain varieties are highly desirable, though. In late spring or early summer, long, dangling clusters of creamy white, fragrant flowers develop, persisting for a week or two. The foliage is dark green, with the pinnately compound leaves consisting of many small leaflets. On older specimens the rough, plated, grayish brown, deeply fissured bark is attractive year-round.

Black locust may establish in many different sites, but it thrives best in moist, well-drained soil and full sun or partial shade. The recommended varieties below make great specimens and act a focal points in the garden. Hardy from Zones 4–8.

NOTABLE VARIETIES
Black locust is difficult to find commercially, but certain varieties are well worth pursuing.

'Frisia'. This excellent fast-growing variety has ferny foliage that emerges golden yellow in spring and changes to a chartreuse green in midsummer. This variety is a wonderful accent in mid- to late summer against an evergreen background. The foliage somewhat hides the white flowers, although the floral display is respectable. 'Frisia' is a very vigorous, upright-growing tree to 40 ft. tall and half the spread.

'Lace Lady' (Twisty Baby). This peculiar form of black locust has twisted stems and branches. It rarely flowers, but the gnarled habit and dense foliage is quite attractive. 'Lace Lady' grows 10–15 ft. tall and can be used as a focal point in the garden.

'Purple Robe'. This variety offers large clusters of showy, rosy pink flowers, which contrast well against the dark green foliage.

Sophora (Styphnolobium) japonica
Japanese pagoda tree, scholar tree

Although the beautiful Japanese pagoda tree grows larger than the average residential landscape can accommodate, it truly deserves honorable mention as a flowering tree that also offers shade in the summer.

Even from a distance the scholar tree, as it is sometimes called, is very recognizable when in full bloom, brightening up the green summer landscape. The large, airy, creamy yellow flower clusters, which open in mid- to late summer, contrast nicely against the dark foliage. They fill the air with a pleasant fragrance, making the entire pagoda tree hum with the sound of bees, which will flock to the flowers even as they fall to the ground.

The Japanese pagoda tree's lacy pinnately compound, dark green foliage and rounded, dense growth habit is attractive from spring until fall. The long, beadlike, translucent, greenish yellow fruit clusters persist well into the fall. The fruit can be rather messy, so siting near a pathway or driveway is not recommended.

Japanese pagoda tree thrives in well-drained, moist, acidic soil and full sun but is very adaptable. It does need space to grow, however, as it can reach 50 ft. or more tall, with a similar spread. Only the homeowner with enough space should even consider such a large tree.

Japanese pagoda tree is normally used in urban settings and parks. It can also be used in a lawn area or as a shade tree, provided it is sited away from patios, walkways, and driveways (because of the fruit). Hardy from Zones 4–7.

NOTABLE VARIETIES

'Pendula'. A weeping variety that grows only 10–12 ft. tall, it offers a graceful, flowing growth habit but will not flower reliably.

'Regent'. An excellent variety that blooms at an early age, 'Regent' has a dense, rounded habit and improved vigor over the species.

{ *Sorbus alnifolia*
Korean mountain ash

Though my list of favorite flowering trees keeps growing, Korean mountain ash is certainly near the top. Korean mountain ash is a great example of what a flowering tree should be, offering unrivaled aesthetic value all four seasons of the year, cultural adaptability, and excellent landscape function.

Unlike European mountain ash (*S. aucuparia*), Korean mountain ash is resistant to diseases and insects. This Asian native displays 2–3 in. wide, showy clusters of white flowers in spring. The entire tree will be covered with puffs of white for a week or two. The bright green, pleated foliage darkens to deep green by midsummer and turns brilliant shades of yellow, orange, or golden brown in fall. Pinkish red fruit clusters ripen in late summer and persist until late fall or early winter. The combination of fall foliage and red fruit is nothing short of spectacular.

The upright, pyramidal to oval habit and smooth gray bark give Korean mountain ash an unmistakable presence in the landscape, especially in winter. It can grow 40–50 ft. tall and 30 ft. wide but typically ranges from 30–40 ft. tall and 15–20 ft. wide.

Korean mountain ash prefers moist, organic, acidic, well-drained soil but is very adaptable to soils and pH levels. It thrives in full sun or partial shade. Try not to site it in excessively hot, windy sites.

Korean mountain ash works well as a single-specimen lawn tree or in groupings. It will undoubtedly enhance any area of the landscape that it grows in. Hardy from Zones 3–7.

Korean mountain ash flowers

Upright, dense habit of Korean mountain ash

{ *Staphylea trifolia*
American bladdernut

American bladdernut is a little-known native large shrub or small tree growing in the wilds of eastern Canada to the midwestern and southeastern United States. At maturity it will form dense habit to 15 ft. tall. Although not overwhelming, the small, greenish white, bell-shaped flowers in spring are interesting. In late summer an inflated, papery, light green fruit capsule forms, eventually turning brown. The dark green, trifoliate foliage turns dull yellow in the fall. The smooth, greenish gray bark is highlighted by white stripes and is interesting in the winter.

Bladdernut prefers moist, well-drained soil and full sun or partial shade. It is relatively pest free. Quite adaptable, it will develop a more open habit in shade.

Bladdernut is very effective in a naturalistic, woodland setting. Bladdernut can be used as a single specimen or in small groupings. Hardy from Zones 4–8. Though not often readily available commercially, it can be obtained through specialty and mail-order sources.

Stewartia spp.
Stewartias

Like *Sorbus* and *Aesculus, Stewartia* is at the top of my list of favorite of flowering tree genera. And like *Viburnum,* I have never met a *Stewartia* I didn't like. It is truly royalty among flowering trees. *Stewartia* in general is one of the loveliest flowering trees available to the avid gardener. It boggles my mind that this incredibly diverse genus is not grown and planted more often in American landscapes. A *Stewartia* will undoubtedly provide many years of enjoyment to the gardener who can appreciate its infinite beauty.

Stewartia pseudocamellia (Japanese stewartia)

Like a faithful old friend, Japanese stewartia can always be counted on to brighten the day. This four-season beauty is never dull in the landscape. With outstanding flowers, foliage, fall color, and bark interest, Japanese stewartia clearly ranks in the elite group of flowering trees.

Japanese stewartia offers white flowers in summer, intense foliage color in fall, and exquisite multicolored bark that is interesting twelve months of the year. In early summer the flower buds emerge, resembling large pearls, before opening to pure white flowers with bright yellow centers. The flower is generally 2–3 in.

White flowers of *Stewartia*

across, and blooming will continue sporadically for several weeks to a month. In the fall the dark green foliage changes to brilliant shades of yellow-bronze, orange, red, and maroon, also lasting for several weeks. The fall foliage colors of Japanese stewartia are usually nothing short of spectacular.

But the most ornamental asset of this tree is the smooth, peeling, multicolored bark, which exhibits shades of tan, brown, gray, and beige all year. In winter, Japanese stewartia glistens in the landscape, with its extraordinarily colorful trunk and stems. It is truly one of the most noticeable trees for winter interest. The overall growth habit of the Japanese stewartia is gener-

© Bruce Curtis

Multicolored bark of *Stewartia*

© Bruce Curtis

Deep reddish orange fall color of *Stewartia*

ally pyramidal when young, more open and broad with age. It can reach 20–30 ft. tall, with a slightly smaller spread. It can get larger, but it rarely does in the cultivated garden setting.

Japanese stewartia is a carefree tree that is ideal for the home garden. Although related to *Franklinia*, Japanese stewartia is easier to grow and more reliable in the residential landscape. *Stewartia* is pest free and prefers full sun or partial shade and well-drained, acidic, moist soil. I have witnessed this tree performing admirably even in dense shade. Even though a young specimen can be impressive, a newly planted Japanese stewartia does need a few years to become established. But Japanese stewartia is indeed worth the wait; this choice flowering tree will only get better with age. It has a medium to slow growth rate and will eventually develop into a dense, upright tree.

© Vincent A. Simeone

Upright habit and bronzy yellow fall color of *Stewartia*

Japanese stewartia should be sited in a highly visible area of the garden. It is a quintessential specimen flowering tree, suitable for a woodland garden or a lawn area or as a companion plant to rhododendrons, azaleas, and other flowering shrubs. It is hardy from Zones 4–7, but it needs protection in Zone 4.

NOTABLE VARIETIES
'Ballet'. Beautiful, graceful branches, large white flowers, and orange-brown fall color set this variety apart from the others.

'Milk and Honey'. A vigorous grower with large, 3 in. diameter creamy white flowers and reddish tan bark. A very floriferous plant.

Other *Stewartia* species
There are several worthy species of *Stewartia* for the garden besides *S. pseudocamellia*, and all of them offer superior garden merit. *S. koreana*, Korean stewartia, is very similar to Japanese stewartia, with the exception of the fall color and bark characteristics. Some experts contend that Korean stewartia has superior exfoliating bark and more vibrant red fall color. Korean stewartia is strongly pyramidal and dense even as a mature tree. It will grow 20–30 ft. tall, with about half the spread. Hardy from Zones 5–7.

Stewartia malacodendron, silky stewartia, is native to the southeastern United States. This is a fairly unknown species in commerce, but once seen in flower, the passionate gardener will move mountains to obtain it. Truly a breathtaking sight in flower! This small tree, which will reach 10–15 ft. tall, features striking white flowers with purple centers in mid- to late summer. It has a gray-brown bark that is attractive but not as ornamental as other *Stewartia* species.

Silky stewartia is quite finicky and needs very well-drained soil in order to survive. It also prefers evenly moist soil, a light layer of mulch, and partial shade. The cool, dappled light from overhead trees will benefit this tree in the hot summer months. It is hardy from Zones 7–9, but it will survive in Zone 6 with protection.

Another native of the southeastern United States, *S. ovata*, mountain stewartia, offers showy white flowers that range from 2–4 in. in diameter. The bark is not particularly showy compared with other species, but it is still interesting, offering shades of gray and brown and a rough, ridged, and furrowed texture with age.

Mountain stewartia does not grow particularly large, only 10–15 ft. tall with a slightly smaller spread. The habit is somewhat shrubby and is very useful in a garden with limited space. Like most stewartia, mountain stewartia prefers rich, moist, organic, acidic soil. Full sun or partial shade is preferred, and dappled shade during the heat of the afternoon is ideal. This species should be planted as a young tree since it is rather difficult to transplant when older.

Mountain stewartia is an excellent understory tree in a woodland, or it can be used as a single specimen in a garden setting among other ornamental trees and shrubs. Hardy from Zones 5–8.

Stewartia monadelpha, tall stewartia, is an upright, pyramidal flowering tree to 25 ft. tall. The bark on young trees is scaly and exfoliates to expose smooth underbark. On older trees the bark becomes a rich cinnamon brown and is quite smooth. The small, dark green leaves turn reddish maroon in the fall. Although tall stewartia offers the smallest flowers of any species in this discussion—reaching up to 1½ in. in diameter—they are still of fine ornamental quality. The flowers are white with yellow centers.

Tall stewartia is best in partial shade, but it also will grow in full sun with adequate moisture. This species is considered one of the most heat tolerant. Tall stewartia is ideal as a small woodland tree among shade-loving perennials, flowering shrubs, and evergreens. It is hardy from Zones 6–8, but it will grow in Zone 5 with protection.

Stewartia rostrata is a somewhat rare eastern Chinese species that closely resembles the native *S. ovata* but is easier to grow. *S. rostrata* is the first *Stewartia* species to bloom in spring. The 2 in. diameter, white flowers are surrounded by large reddish bracts. The habit is upright and somewhat shrubby, and *S. rostrata* grows to 15 ft. tall. The rough gray-brown bark is also interesting. Hardy from Zones 6–7.

Stewartia serrata, sawtooth stewartia, is one of the first stewartias to bloom in the early summer with 2 in. diameter white blooms with a reddish base. This small, 20–25 ft. tree also offers dark green, leathery leaves that turn a rich reddish color in the fall and beautiful, peeling brown bark. Although not well known, if it's a stewartia, it has to be good. A native of Japan, it is hardy from Zones 5–7.

Stewartia sinensis, Chinese stewartia, is another interesting Asian species. I first witnessed the beauty of this tree at Wakehurst Place in England, where a mature specimen mesmerized me with its stunning light tan, polished bark. Young plants exhibit long, rough sheets of cinnamon brown exfoliating bark, exposing the beautiful underbark. The bark interest on this plant is a thing of sheer beauty. The small, cup-shaped white flowers offer a subtle display and pleasant fragrance. The deep green leaves turn rich shades of red in the fall.

Chinese stewartia is an excellent specimen tree to 25 ft. tall. It is ideal as a single-specimen lawn tree and can also be effective in a woodland setting. It prefers moist, acidic, well-drained soil and full sun or partial shade. *Stewartia sinensis* is hardy from Zones 5–7 and does not like hot, humid climates. This species is not easy to obtain and is usually sought after by the passionate, curious gardener looking for rare and unusual plants to collect.

Styrax spp.
Snowbells
Styrax japonicus (Japanese snowbell)

Japanese snowbell is a pleasant small flowering tree with delicate, lustrous, dark green foliage; white, bell-shaped spring blooms; and smooth, gray-brown bark. The fall foliage is usually not overwhelming, but can be yellow or tinged with reddish purple. The small, white, slightly fragrant flowers look like nodding bells and occur in small clusters along each stem. A small, oval fruit forms and will persist until fall. Japanese snowbell can reach 20–30 ft. tall, with an equal spread. Older specimens develop very attractive smooth, gray bark with deep fissures, making this tree very handsome in the winter landscape.

© Bruce Curtis

Textured bark of an old snowbell tree

Clusters of white flowers of Japanese snowbell

© Bruce Curtis

Japanese snowbell prefers moist, organic, acidic, well-drained soil and full sun or partial shade. In warmer climates it is recommended that trees be sited in partial shade, away from the hot sun.

Japanese snowbell is an excellent specimen tree for a lawn area or a shade garden, and it can also be an excellent companion to rhododendrons, dogwoods, hollies, and other acid-loving woody plants. Hardy from Zones 5–8.

NOTABLE VARIETIES
'Angyo Dwarf'. This is a lovely small tree with a dwarf habit to 10 ft. tall. The flowers and other ornamental features are similar to those of the species.

'Carillon', also known as 'Pendula'. One of the most handsome weeping flowering trees, this tree offers a graceful, cascading growth habit. It can ultimately reach 12 ft. tall.

'Crystal'. The habit of this flowering tree is upright and fastigiate. 'Crystal' has dark green foliage and white flowers that dangle from purplish pedicels (stems).

'Emerald Pagoda'. This variety offers superior, large flowers and thick, dark green, leathery leaves. The habit is upright and vase shaped when the tree is young. A very striking selection.

'Pink Chimes'. Considered superior to 'Rosea', this pink-flowered form offers striking flowers that do not fade.

'Rosea'. A pink selection with clear pink flowers and a distinctly dwarf growth habit.

Styrax obassia (fragrant snowbell)
Similar in stature to Japanese snowbell, the fragrant snowbell (*Styrax obassia*) offers several different ornamental features. The small, noticeably fragrant, white, bell-shaped flowers are borne in long, dangling clusters along each stem. The lush, broad, dark green leaves and hanging clusters of flowers are noticeably different than those of Japanese snowbell. Although the fall foliage is not usually striking, pleasant shades of yellow or yellow-green can be observed. The smooth, gray-brown bark is also very handsome and is especially noticeable in winter. The growth habit is pyramidal to oval, reaching 30 ft. tall.

Fragrant snowbell prefers moist, organic, acidic, well-drained soil and partial shade. It will also grow

© Bruce Curtis

Lush foliage and white flowers of fragrant snowbell

well in full sun, but adequate moisture should be provided in times of drought. This tree is not particularly good in hot, exposed sites.

Fragrant snowbell is an excellent single-specimen lawn tree and is exceptionally effective in a shaded, woodland setting. Hardy from Zones 5–8.

Symplocos paniculata
Sapphireberry

A rather obscure small tree, sapphireberry is native to the Himalayas, China, and Japan. In late spring beautiful creamy white, fragrant flowers form in 2–3 in. long clusters called panicles. Striking glossy, bright turquoise blue fruit ripens in the fall. The fruit offers a very unique, attractive display late in the growing season and will attract birds to the garden. The hand-

some, dark green leaves do not offer any appreciable fall color. As this small tree matures, the thick gray stems become ridged and furrowed, displaying interesting texture and color in the winter.

Sapphireberry can reach 10–20 ft. tall, with a similar spread. This relatively tough tree is quite adaptable, being tolerant of heat, drought, and pests, but it thrives in moist, well-drained soil and full sun or partial shade. Pruning can be done during the winter months while the plant is dormant.

Sapphireberry can be used as a single-specimen but is best in a small grouping, which will encourage cross-pollination and more reliable fruit displays. Hardy from Zones 4–8.

Syringa reticulata
Japanese tree lilac

Although lilacs are best known for their sweetly fragrant white, purple, or pink spring flowers, Japanese tree lilac is valued for its four seasons of interest. An upright, small to medium-size tree, Japanese tree lilac displays plumes of fragrant white flowers in late spring or early summer. The dense, puffy flower clusters often reach 6– 12 in. long and will persist for several weeks. The leaves will remain dark green all summer; the foliage does not develop striking fall color, although it may be tinged with purple. Among the most unique features of this handsome small tree are its dark brown bark and vase-shaped growth habit. The bark, with noticeable lenticels resembling those of cherry or birch bark, is quite noticeable in winter and contrasts nicely against a snowy background.

Puffy, white flowers of Japanese tree lilac

© Bruce Curtis

Upright habit of Japanese tree lilac

© Bruce Curtis

Japanese tree lilac prefers full sun, although it is tolerant of partial shade. It also prefers moist, well-drained soil but is adaptable to varying soil textures and degrees of pH. It will tolerate dry, sandy soils as well as heavy clay soils. Japanese tree lilac can be vulnerable to common lilac pests, and some maintenance may be required. For a lilac, however, this species is very durable and fairly resistant to pests and diseases.

Japanese tree lilac is ideal as a single-specimen tree and in groupings, and it has even been used as a street tree. It will grow 20–30 ft. tall, with about half the spread. Hardy from Zones 3–7.

NOTABLE VARIETIES

'Cameo Jewel'. This is a new variegated form with yellow-cream–splashed foliage.

'Chantilly Lace'. This variety offers variegated foliage, with leaf margins a pale, creamy yellow. It should be sited in a partially shaded location out of direct afternoon sun.

'Ivory Silk'. This selection forms a pleasant, rounded tree, with stocky branch structure, to 25 ft. tall. It is very common in commerce and blooms heavily, even as a young plant. The healthy, dark green leaves are not bothered by pests, and the cherryesque bark is attractive all year.

'Summer Snow'. A more compact, rounded tree reaching up to 20 ft. tall, this lilac produces a profusion of very large flower panicles. Its toughness and small size make this variety ideal as a street tree.

{ *Tetradium daniellii*
Korean evodia

Korean evodia has undergone a name change recently and is still largely found under its former taxonomic name: *Evodia daniellii*. This may be confusing because I am sure it will continue to be called Korean evodia, not Korean tetradium. Korean evodia is also nicknamed the bee tree because the creamy white clusters of summer flowers attract bees—on a sunny summer day entire trees will literally be buzzing with activity. The lustrous, dark green, pinnately compound leaves turn yellow in fall. The most impressive feature of Korean evodia is the deep reddish purple fruit clusters, which burst open to expose shiny, jet black seed. The ornamental fruit display starts in late summer and continues into the fall. Fall foliage color varies from year to year from a muted greenish yellow to bright yellow and offers a nice contrast to the fruit. The smooth, gray bark is also very handsome and offers winter interest.

Korean evodia prefers moist, well-drained soil and full sun or partial shade. It is quite adaptable to vari-

Korean evodia fruit display

ous soil types and can tolerate poor soil, provided it is well drained.

Few flowering trees offer as much late-summer and fall interest as evodia. It is an excellent specimen tree in a lawn area. Several of the largest specimens I have ever witnessed, in Old Westbury, New York, are 40 ft. tall and 50 ft. wide. Typically, though, Korean evodia will get 20–30 ft. tall and wide. Hardy from Zones 4–8.

{ *Viburnum* spp.
Tree-type viburnums

Although there are many delightful species and varieties of *Viburnum* that are excellent flowering shrubs, there are also several species that can be grown as small trees. Like their shrubby relatives, tree-type viburnums offer several seasons of interest, cultural adaptability, and unlimited landscape function. The species discussed in this section display an upright, rigid growth habit, showy white flowers, bluish black fruit, reddish purple fall foliage, and interesting grayish brown bark. These tree-type viburnums may be a bit more difficult to find in commerce, but they make great additions to the landscape.

Viburnum prunifolium (blackhaw viburnum)

Blackhaw viburnum is a small flowering tree with stiff branches and a rounded canopy. Its dense, layered habit looks similar to that of hawthorn (*Crataegus* spp.) in the landscape as it matures, and larger specimens can be quite interesting all year. Although somewhat slow to become established, blackhaw viburnum is worth the wait. It offers interesting flowers, lush foliage, colorful fall foliage, showy fruit displays, and rough, light brown bark.

Interesting creamy white, flat-topped flowers emerge in spring and persist for several weeks. The flower display can be quite profuse, effective even from a distance. During the summer lush, deep green, smooth leaves offer a pleasant texture. The leaves change to bronze, purple, or deep red in the fall and can be striking. Also in the fall, the clusters of pinkish red fruit ripen to deep black-

Creamy white flowers of blackhaw viburnum

ish purple. The fruit is a tasty treat for birds. The dense, rounded habit and rough-textured, gray-brown bark adds winter interest in the landscape. Mature plants can reach 15–25 ft. high, with a similar spread.

Blackhaw viburnum prefers moist, well-drained soil and full sun but will also perform well in partial shade. It is very adaptable to soil types and is especially good in dry soil. Blackhaw viburnum is relatively pest free and will perform well in a wide variety of landscape environments.

Blackhaw viburnum is an excellent small specimen tree for a woodland setting or a lawn area. It can also be used in small groupings. This very useful plant should be used more often in both residential and commercial settings. Hardy from Zones 3–9.

NOTABLE VARIETY
'Early Red'. The new foliage in the spring is tinged red, and the fall foliage develops a rich burgundy.

Viburnum rufidulum (rusty blackhaw viburnum)
As its name suggests, rusty blackhaw viburnum (*Viburnum rufidulum*) is closely related to blackhaw viburnum, and it also possesses exceptional garden merit. In many respects this southern species is very similar to *V. prunifolium*, but the stems, buds, and leaf undersides are covered with dark rusty brown pubescence, or hairs. It offers lustrous, dark green, leathery foliage, which turns rich burgundy tones as cold weather approaches in the autumn. The creamy white flowers, bluish black fruit with a bloomy coating, and rough, brown, dogwoodlike bark make this species a real winner.

Rusty blackhaw viburnum will grow 10–20 ft. tall under cultivated landscape conditions. This rather obscure species should be embraced by the avid gardener. Hardy from Zones 5–9.

Viburnum sieboldii (Siebold viburnum)
Several *Viburnum* species grow into large shrubs or small trees. One of the most popular is the Siebold viburnum. This large-scale plant, with its large, oblong leaves, adds bold texture to the landscape. The leaves are a dark, lustrous green with very pronounced veins. Creamy white, flat-topped flowers emerge at the end of each branch in spring. The leaves smell like burnt rubber if rubbed and have been reported as deer resistant because of the foliage's pungent odor. The glossy, bright red fruit clusters change to black in late summer or early fall and provide an enjoyable meal for birds. The overall growth pattern is upright and dense at youth and eventually reaches 15–20 ft. high.

© Vincent A. Simeone

Lush foliage and creamy flower of Siebold viburnum

Upright, dense habit of Siebold viburnum

Deep red fruit of Siebold viburnum

reminds me of kousa dogwood in bloom because of its profusion of white flowers and its layered growth habit. This species is one of the first in summer to display colorful fruit, which various species of birds enjoy. The deeply ridged leaves provide wonderful texture during the summer and turn red or maroon in fall.

Doublefile viburnum has a uniquely graceful growth habit, with the lateral branches typically growing in a horizontal arrangement. It can reach 10–12 ft. tall, with a slightly wider spread. Once established, this large shrub or small tree will make an impressive specimen and become the focal point of the garden. It is also very effective in small groupings. Doublefile viburnum does best from Zones 5–7, but it will grow in Zone 8 with adequate moisture and specific siting.

Siebold viburnum is an adaptable plant, but it does prefer well-drained, moist soil and full sun or partial shade. It is rather heat and drought tolerant once established. It is an excellent small specimen tree for a home garden and is also effective in mass plantings and as a screen. Hardy from Zones 4–8.

Viburnum plicatum var. *tomentosum* (doublefile viburnum)

One of the most popular and versatile viburnums for the home garden, doublefile viburnum got its name from the double rows of white flowers that line up along the stems like soldiers at attention. Flat, white, lace-cap–like flowers emerge in midspring and transform into deep red fruit in mid- to late summer. This viburnum

Showy white flowers of doublefile viburnum

Layered branching of doublefile viburnum

© Vincent A. Simeone

NOTABLE VARIETIES

'Mariesii'. This excellent, reliable performer has large white flowers, beautiful red fruit, and superior red fall color. Its distinctly horizontal branching habit distinguishes this plant from all of the others in the garden.

'Molly Schroeder'. A new selection, this viburnum has pink flowers in spring. If growing conditions permit, it may sporadically rebloom in the fall, providing another show.

'Shasta'. This is a wide-spreading selection, reaching 12 ft. wide and 6–8 ft. tall. Large, showy flowers, bright red fruit, and purple-maroon fall foliage make 'Shasta' a garden gem!

'Shoshoni'. Similar to 'Shasta' but on a smaller scale, it grows to only 5 ft. in height, making it appropriate for the small landscape, the perennial border, and foundation planting.

'Summer Snowflake'. This truly dwarf plant is smaller in size and overall stature than most doublefile viburnum varieties, reaching only 6–8 ft. tall. It flowers heavily for the first few weeks, then sporadically but continuously through the summer and into the autumn. This very well-behaved plant also offers showy red fruit.

The dramatic flower and fruit of 'Summer Snowflake'

Vitex agnus-castus
Chastetree

Chastetree is a summer-blooming large shrub or small tree with fine, palm-shaped leaves and long spikes of violet-blue flowers. The 12–18 in. long flower spikes emerge in midsummer and continue through early fall. The dark, grayish green foliage adds a beautiful lacy texture to the garden, as well. This plant tends to get larger in southern gardens than in colder climates.

Regular annual pruning—though not completely necessary—will keep your chastetree compact and floriferous. It blooms on the current season's growth, so

it can be cut down to 6–12 in. from the ground early in the spring. The shrub will grow back several feet in one season, with a dense, manageable growth habit, and produce masses of flowers. However, if a tree form is what you desire, this type of pruning should not be done unless absolutely necessary. If left unpruned, chastetree can reach 15–20 ft. tall, with a similar spread.

Chastetree is a fast-growing plant that prefers moist, well-drained soil and full sun. It is slow to leaf out in the spring but will flourish in hot weather. It thrives in hot, dry locations and is quite drought tolerant. Chastetree can be used very similarly to butterfly bush

© Bruce Curtis

Chastetree in flower

in mass plantings or as an effective backdrop to perennials. As a tree it can be used as a single specimen or in small groupings. I have seen this plant growing in deer-infested areas with little or no browsing damage, so I suspect this is an additional attribute. Chastetree is hardy from Zones 6–9, but it performs best in Zones 7 and 8.

A similar species, *Vitex negundo*, can also grow 15–20 ft. tall. Its main difference from *V. agnus-castus* is its smaller, bluish purple or lilac flowers. It is also slightly more cold hardy, performing well to Zone 5 with protection.

NOTABLE VARIETIES

'Abbeville Blue'. This excellent selection has deep blue flowers.

'Alba'. This variety has attractive white flowers, providing a bright accent to the landscape.

'Silver Spire'. This vigorous grower offers large, pure white flowers.

Site Selection and Tree Care

The keys to a successful garden are proper planning and selecting the right plant for your specific needs. By placing the right plant in the right place, many garden pitfalls can be avoided. A well-designed garden is both functional and aesthetically pleasing.

Before selecting flowering trees, it is essential that the gardener understand some key factors about the landscape, such as soil type, light exposure, and specific environmental conditions, such as wind. In addition, knowing the cultural requirements of your tree purchase candidates is vital to choosing ones that will succeed. Adequate soil moisture, pruning, fertilization, and proper planting procedures are all important aspects of gardening to consider. By correctly assessing growing conditions and understanding the needs of specific flowering trees, the gardener can make sound decisions on plants that will thrive in the garden. All too often plants are purchased and simply planted wherever they fit, with no real consideration of their cultural requirements or ultimate size. Proper care of your landscape will result in healthy, productive, and beautiful flowering trees that will offer years of enjoyment.

Soil

Soil is probably one of the most overlooked but essential factors when choosing flowering trees. Knowing your soil type, drainage, and pH is critical to a successful garden. Garden soil can vary greatly in many areas of the United States. It is essential that you test your soil pH and determine your soil's texture before planting. Soil texture and composition can range from heavy, clay soil to well-drained, loamy soil to light, sandy soil. These basic classes represent the ability of different types of soil to retain moisture and nutrients. Though most of the trees discussed in this book perform best in moist but well-drained soil, some flowering trees need special conditions or can tolerate a wide variety of soils.

Soil pH (its relative acidity or alkalinity) is an important factor. Certain plant groups, such as dogwoods, prefer acidic soil, whereas other flowering trees will perform well in neutral or alkaline soil. Soil pH is measured on a scale from 1 to 14, in which 7.0 is neutral. Soil pH below 7.0 is considered acidic; soil pH above 7.0 is alkaline. Soil pH meters or test kits, which can be purchased in a local garden center or nursery, will allow you to determine the pH of your garden soil. In addition, soil samples can be brought to your local extension service for testing. Soil testing may also provide valuable diagnostic and treatment information for existing flowering trees that are not performing well in your landscape.

Soil pH can be raised or lowered by adding products to the soil. For example, garden lime (calcium carbonate) can be added to raise the pH, whereas aluminum sulfate will acidify soil. Such natural products as manure and compost also generally acidify the soil. Soil pH should be altered gradually, over an extended period of time, however, so only a limited amount of such products can be added to soil at one time. It is important to read the directions located on these products' packaging.

Light Exposure

Light exposure, how sunny or shady your garden is, plays an important role in the success of your flowering trees. There are three basic types of natural light in the garden: full sun, partial shade, or shade—with variations of each. Certain trees prefer full sun, whereas others need the protection provided by taller trees overhead.

You can determine the types of light exposure in various parts of your garden by closely monitoring the sunlight from hour to hour. This is generally best done in early summer (June 21), when the sun is strongest. This test can also be performed through July with accurate results. Garden areas that receive at least five or six hours of direct sunlight a day are considered *full sun* sites. Fewer hours than that are considered different degrees of shade, from light to dense. *Partial shade* is where plants receive about four hours or less of sun, either direct or indirect, per day. In partial

shade, if the plants do get direct sun, it is usually early or late in the day, coming in at a low angle under the canopy of tall trees. *Shade* refers to an area of the garden in no direct sun, or in partial darkness. It is crucial to know which level of sunlight you have in your garden before siting your trees.

Wind Exposure

It is important to know the amount of wind that different sections of your garden experience. Certain trees will tolerate wind better than others. High wind exposure is often found in seashore environments along coastal areas. High winds can also be experienced in open, flat plains or along exposed mountainsides with little or no shelter. In such cases, only a select group of plants that will tolerate these exposed conditions can be chosen. For example, dogwoods and magnolias are not particularly tolerant of windy sites, but crabapples, hawthorns, and pears are. In the home garden, if high winds are problematic on a seasonal basis, it may be prudent to site your sensitive flowering trees in areas where fences, buildings, or even select evergreen screens can protect them. Incorporating different types of shrubs, evergreens, and flowering trees together can be beneficial to all of them, since they complement each other.

Selecting the Right Trees

Once you have determined the soil, light exposure, wind conditions, and any other important characteristics of the garden, important issues concerning flowering tree selection must be addressed. You must first determine what you are hoping to accomplish when using a tree in the garden. What is the desired function of the tree? Do you need a strategically placed specimen tree for an accent of spring color? A grouping of small trees to screen an unsightly view? A very small tree near the foundation of your house to add interest?

What colors and textures are you interested in introducing into the garden? How will a new tree look with other existing plant material? And, most important, will the tree you have chosen outgrow the space you have selected for it? Putting a tree in too small of a site will only lead to problems in the future. More trees and shrubs have been butchered to make them fit a space than I care to think about.

Answering a few simple questions and taking some time to properly plan your garden planting project will most certainly ensure success. It is part of the journey of the gardener.

Proper Planting

It is imperative that proper planting techniques be applied with when planting or transplanting trees. It is not enough simply to dig a hole and place soil around the root-ball of the plant. Special care must be taken in preparing the planting site. This planning will ensure that your valuable tree will thrive in its new setting. It is also very important to understand that generally, the larger the tree, the longer it takes to become established in its new home, due to transplant shock. As a general rule for larger transplanted trees, for every inch of tree caliper (diameter of the main trunk), a tree needs one year of aftercare. That is, the new transplant needs to be watered, fertilized, and otherwise monitored for that period of time. So, a 4 in. caliper flowering cherry should receive TLC for four growing seasons.

Several important steps should be followed when planting a flowering tree. The best time to plant a flowering tree is in spring or fall while the air temperature is cool and the soil is moist. Exact timing depends on the specific climate where you live and the species of tree being planted. No planting should be done during the extremes of summer or winter. Overall, I think most deciduous flowering trees are best planted in the spring, with the fall season as a good second choice. In many cases, the best nursery stock is available in the spring because the gardening season is young.

Again, you have selected your plant with consideration of the garden soil's characteristics. Specific location is important, too, depending on the tree's purpose in your garden's overall scheme and its requirements for light and protection from the elements. Of course, be sure to site your flowering tree in an area of the garden where it will have plenty of room to grow.

> "He who plants a tree
> Plants a hope."
> —*Lucy Larcom (1824–93),*
> *in "Plant a Tree"*

Now the planting hole can be prepared. The size of the hole depends on the size of the root ball. When a tree or shrub is purchased from a plant nursery, it is typically growing as a balled-and-burlapped (B&B) plant or in a container. Burlap is a rough cloth material that covers and supports the roots and soil of a plant, perhaps with help from rope, wire, or plastic, until future planting in another location. Containers can range in size and type but are often made of plastic. In either case, the planting hole should be at least three times as wide as the diameter of the root ball. This will allow the roots to become established in loose, fluffy soil.

It is very important that your tree be placed at the proper depth in the soil. This is without a doubt the most common mistake made. Trees that are planted too deeply are doomed to fail; they often decline slowly, but they will eventually succumb. When planting your new tree, the top of the root ball should be even with or slightly above the soil level. With a B&B purchase, peel back the top of the burlap to check the exact level of the top of the root ball; the rest of the burlap should probably stay in place during these early stages of the planting procedure to help hold the root ball together. As a general rule I recommend placing the tree so that the top of the root ball is about 1 in. above the soil line in case of settling.

Be sure the root ball soil itself isn't built up too high on the trunk. Trees have what is known as a root flare, the bulging area where the tree trunk meets the soil (see illustration). Most trees, with few exceptions, have a root flare, which is usually most evident in trees with trunks

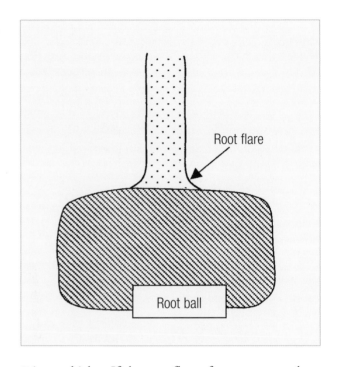

2 in. or thicker. If the root flare of your new purchase is not visible, it could be an indication that soil is covering it. Gently remove soil from the root ball closest to the base of the trunk to expose the root flare. Once you've done this, situating the tree in the planting hole will be easy. Make sure that the tree does not settle too low in the planting hole, which might allow the flare to become covered again when you fill in the hole.

These root flare tips can also help you with an established tree that is planted too deeply or that has had soil accumulate against its trunk over time. Again, gently remove any soil from the trunk to expose the root flare.

Once you've got the root ball and tree sitting at the right height in the hole, remove as much rope, plastic,

Tree Planting Detail for Trees up to 6-in. Caliper

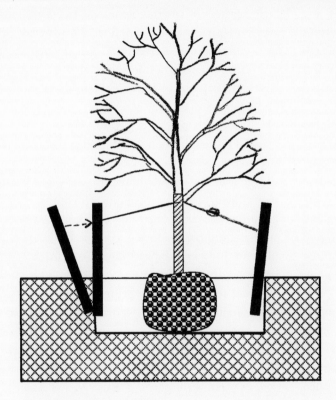

Guidelines for Planting a Tree up to 6-In. Caliper

1. Dig the hole at least three times the width of the root ball.

2. Set the root ball on firm, undisturbed soil.

3. When the tree is safely placed in the ground, cut and remove the top third of any wire basket. Also, remove all nylon ropes, burlap, and straps that may be attached to the root ball.

4. Backfill the planting hole with soil.

5. Top dress with 1½ in. of shredded mulch.

6. The top of the root ball should be flush or slightly above grade to expose the root flare. The root flare should be visible when finished planting.

7. Water regularly after planting.

Steps to Staking a Tree

a. Using 3 ft. long, 3 in. diameter milled cedar or 4 in. diameter natural cedar stakes (two per tree), dive the stakes in at an angle and draw vertical to the tree with wire to create tension.

b. A nylon strap or reinforced rubber hose should be secured above the first branch.

c. Use a ³⁄₁₆ in. galvanized turnbuckle to secure the wire to the tree.

d. Stakes should be removed after one year.

wire, burlap, and so on as possible from the planting hole to ensure proper growth. It is very important, though, not to break or damage the root ball in any way. Leaning or standing on the root ball is a serious error. If removal of all of the burlap or wire basket is not possible without damaging the root ball, which is usually the case, carefully remove this material from just the top third to half of the root ball.

At the time of purchase, make sure to ask your nursery professional which type of burlap is on your plant's root ball. Some burlap may be treated with a product that inhibits it from decaying, as often indicated by a green coloration. Treated burlap, if left in the planting hole, may remain relatively intact for many years and interfere with root growth. Therefore, as much treated burlap as possible should be cut out of the planting hole and discarded. Untreated burlap, on the other hand, will naturally break down. Although as much of it as possible should be removed from the planting hole, too, leaving some in is not much of a concern because it will rot fairly quickly underground and not hinder the growth. Container-grown shrubs and trees are handled quite differently from those that are balled and burlapped. In the nursery, a flowering tree growing in a container has very often become pot-bound, meaning that there is a large volume of roots that fill the container. As growing roots reach the side of the pot, they have nowhere to go but around and around, forming a thick mesh. When you pull your new tree and its root ball from the container, you may need to tease out such a fibrous web of roots carefully, or gently slice it apart with a knife to open it up. This will encourage the roots to grow out into the planting site soil.

Regardless of whether your new tree arrives balled and burlapped or in a container, the planting procedure is similar (see illustration). Once the planting hole has been prepared and the tree is set at the appropriate depth, the soil can be backfilled into the planting hole and lightly tamped. Any excess soil, rocks, broken roots or other debris can be discarded. The tree should be watered thoroughly and slowly, so that the entire planting hole is evenly moist. Gently tamping the soil and slowly watering will also remove air pockets in the newly disturbed soil. Depending on your soil type, the planting hole may or may not require soil amendments such as compost, manure, and so on. If the soil you are planting in is well-drained topsoil or garden loam, no soil amendments may be needed. If the soil is sandy or clay and the specific tree being planted benefits from amendments, then compost may be incorporated into the existing soil. Peat moss is not as effective as compost because it does not have significant nutritional value in the soil. When you are amending the soil, I do not recommend drastically changing the soil backfilled into the planting hole. A thin layer of mulch covering the soil around the root ball will reduce soil moisture fluctuations and weed growth. A newly planted tree should be watered regularly for at least two growing seasons to ensure its establishment.

Integrated Pest Management

Integrated pest management, or IPM, is a very important component of a garden maintenance program.

The main goals of IPM are to develop sustainable ways of managing pests effectively and efficiently and to help people to use methods that minimize environmental, health, and economic risks. A successful IPM program incorporates garden monitoring and many forms of pest control, such as biological, cultural, physical or mechanical, and chemical controls, as well as proper plant selection.

The most important factor associated with IPM is monitoring the landscape. A gardener must regularly scout the plants in the landscape to observe the types and quantities of pests that might be present. If a low pest population is observed, no action may be necessary. Once a pest has crossed a certain population or damage threshold or caused some other concern, it may be necessary for the gardener to take action. One excellent way to monitor pest populations is through pest traps, which are usually attractive to insects because of color or scent. Through systematic monitoring of traps, a gardener can pinpoint when a pest has arrived in the garden, how the population is growing, and then decide whether control is justified.

Biological controls are beneficial insects and other organisms that reduce pest numbers, by preying on them or infecting them with a pest-specific disease. Although many beneficial organisms are common insects we can easily recognize, others are microscopic and harder to detect. One good example of an effective beneficial insect that reduces harmful pest populations is the ladybug, which eats aphids. Other beneficial insects include *Encarsia* (a wasp that preys on whitefly), *Cryptolaemus* (mealybug killers), and praying mantis (though a praying mantis may also eat some of the beneficial insects—they are more concerned with their appetite than your garden). Bt—*Bacillus thuringiensis*, a beneficial bacterium—and certain nematodes are examples of microscopic beneficial organisms. Several garden supply companies offer beneficial insects for release into the garden. Biological controls have become very popular because they control pests with little or no need for pesticides.

Physical and mechanical controls are very similar and also require no chemicals. You can personally remove or kill harmful pests simply by taking action. For example, scale can be wiped off plants very easily with just a cloth and rubbing alcohol. Although this physical method is very time consuming, it is also very safe to the plant and the environment. Mechanical control is similar, but it usually involves some type of machinery. Many mechanical devices can help you manage garden pests. For instance, harmful beetles can live and breed in brushpiles and other wood debris. A wood chipper eliminates brush and reduces the beetle population. Or mechanically removing thatch from a lawn with a dethatching device can create a healthier environment for turf by increasing oxygen, water, and nutrient absorption.

Cultural practices, a very important component of IPM, are usually related to reducing disease or insect problems through sanitation or other practices that would enhance a plant's growing conditions. The main goal of using sound cultural practices is to create optimal environmental conditions for plants and to reduce plant stress. This will result in the reduced likelihood of these plants being vulnerable to pest problems. In essence, healthy, thriving plants are generally less susceptible to diseases and insects.

One facet of IPM that is very effective is to plant genetically superior or pest-resistant plants to start with. I believe this is the single most important component of IPM. New varieties of landscape plants and agricultural crops are being developed on a regular basis. These plants are bred for pest resistance, drought tolerance, and improved aesthetic value. Many experts feel that using superior plants in appropriate locations will significantly reduce pest problems and the need for pesticides. Universities have plant evaluation and selection programs to evaluate plants for such purposes. The results of these programs filter down to farmers, nurserymen, retailers, and, eventually, homeowners.

Chemical controls, such as pesticides, are usually considered a last resort in an effective IPM program, which encourages alternatives to pesticides whenever possible. If it seems that all other reasonable means of control have failed and there is no other choice, chemical control can be considered. Be sure to contact your local agricultural extension service or horticultural professional for advice. If a pesticide is needed to control a pest, the environmentally safest, least-harmful product should be considered first. Good examples of lower-toxicity pesticides are horticultural oils and soaps, which break down quickly in the environment, with few lingering residual effects. Before applying any pesticide, it is imperative to read the label carefully.

With proper monitoring and implementation of sound pest management practices, landscapes can be maintained more efficiently and effectively. This creates a productive, safe, and aesthetically pleasing environment for all to enjoy.

Pruning

Proper pruning techniques are important for maintaining healthy, beautiful flowering trees. An ongoing pruning schedule will result in vigorous, productive plants and maximize flowering and fruiting potential.

Several factors must be considered before pruning a flowering tree. The two most important considerations are the type of flowering tree and the desired outcome. Flowering trees are pruned differently than shrubs, and the desired outcome is usually different. While shrubs are often trained as hedges and used in mass plantings, foundation plantings, or in a mixed border, flowering trees are usually utilized as single specimens, in small groupings, or as an allee. For these reasons, and because the habit and growth patterns of flowering trees are unique, pruning practices are quite different. Flowering trees either bloom on the current season's growth, such as a rose of Sharon (*Hibiscus syriacus*) and peegee hydrangea (*Hydrangea paniculata* 'Grandiflora'), or on the previous season's growth, such as cherries (*Prunus* spp.) and crabapples (*Malus* spp.). Pruning a tree that blooms on the current season's growth in early spring, before the onset of new growth, will stimulate the plant to produce foliage and flowers the same season. With a tree that flowers on the previous season's growth, pruning should take place soon after the plant has finished blooming.

As a general rule, pruning to encourage new growth, in late winter or early spring, can be more severe, whereas pruning in the late spring or summer, soon after flowering, should be more modest. Pruning after the flowering cycle should not be severe, because the tree may be damaged. Do not overprune, and only prune if you are sure the plant needs it.

Pruning needs vary among specific plant species and landscape situations. For example, often such fruit trees as crabapples develop a large quantity of suckers and watersprouts, which are vegetative branches that grow from the roots or the main trunk. By removing a percentage of them in summer, their regrowth will be suppressed. Removing one-third of sucker and water sprout growth each year over a three-year period is more effective than removing everything at once.

In general, a younger, more vigorous tree should be pruned more often to train it to develop a good structural habit early on. With any tree, pruning dead, diseased, or broken branches can be done at any time of the year with little negative impact. However, doing this type of pruning in winter is desirable because the plant is dormant and on deciduous trees any problems or issues are easier to see. Remember, though, that pruning late in the season (late summer and fall) can stimulate the tree to grow new, fleshy stems, which are vulnerable to frost and the cold temperatures of autumn.

The three-cut method is the proper way to prune a flowering tree (see illustration). This method, generally used on branches that exceed 1 in. in diameter, will ensure that the branch heals properly. The first cut is made with a pruning saw on the underside of the branch, only partway through the branch and 1–2 ft. from the larger limb or main trunk of the tree. This cut

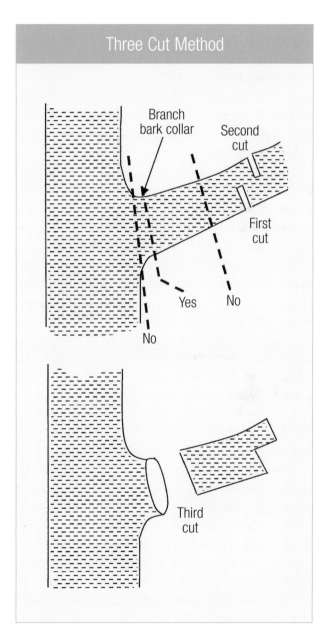

Three Cut Method

will reduce the chance that the next cut, on the branch's topside, will tear off the bark down the larger limb or trunk.

The second cut is made on the top of the limb about 1–2 in. farther out than the first. As the second cut is made, the weight of the branch will cause it to break between the two cuts.

Now, with the majority of the weight lifted from the limb, the third and final cut can be made. Before making this cut, identify the branch bark collar, the swollen area where the branch meets the limb or trunk. Leaving the branch bark collar intact will ensure that the plant properly heals the wound. If the branch is cut either too close to the main stem or trunk, into the collar, or too far from the limb or trunk, proper healing will not occur.

For branches thinner than 1 in. in diameter, hand pruning shears or lopping shears can be used for pruning or removal. Branches of this size do not usually cause problems because they do not weigh much.

Tools

Proper pruning tools are essential for maintaining healthy flowering trees that will produce showy flowers and fruit. Though there are many valuable tools that a gardener may use from time to time, none is more important than hand pruning shears, lopping shears, and a handsaw.

There are several types of hand-held pruners, but a bypass type is the most appropriate. This type of pruner works like scissors, one blade passing by the other, and is effective because it cleanly cuts branches

Essential pruning tools: handsaw, lopping shears, and bypass hand shears (top to bottom)

without crushing them. Anvil-type pruning shears tend to crush stems, which causes damage to the remaining branches.

Lopping shears are long-handled pruners that allow more leverage for cutting larger branches than hand pruners. The handles can be made of metal, wood, or fiberglass, and the blades should also be of the bypass type.

A handheld pruning saw is used to prune large branches that are typically too large for a lopping shear to cut. A sharp, thin saw will enable a gardener to effectively reach tight areas within a large mass of branches.

All tools must be kept sharp, clean, and well oiled. Regular maintenance should be performed to ensure proper tool effectiveness. Failure to properly maintain tools may result in unnecessary damage to your flowering trees, such as from ragged cuts. Poorly made pruning cuts often do not heal properly.

Fertilization and Mulching

Most flowering trees benefit from a fertilization program in spring, fall, or both, using a general-purpose garden fertilizer. There are many general-purpose fertilizer products on the market, such as 10-6-4 or 5-10-5. In addition, organic compost products improve the soil, provide natural fertilizer, and improve the water-holding capacity of the soil. Compost is organic material, such as leaves or manure, that has been aged to create humus. Humus is a brown or black organic substance consisting of partially or wholly decayed vegetable or animal matter; it provides nutrients for plants and increases the ability of soil to retain water. Humus is an excellent form of natural fertilizer that plants can readily use.

Organic fertilizer is one of the best substances for fertilizing plants because it is environmentally friendly and much less likely to damage plants, unlike conventional chemical fertilizers, which can damage plants directly or more gradually through overfertilized soil if applied too heavily. In addition, incorporating compost into the soil when a new tree is installed will help the plant become established because it improves the water-holding capacity of the soil.

After planting your new flowering tree, a circle of mulch on the surface of the soil, at least as wide as the planting hole, will greatly benefit your tree. Even an established tree will benefit from a thin, circular layer of mulch. Mulching is generally recommended about once a year, depending on how fast the material decomposes. The best mulch products are natural organic materials, such as shredded leaves, wood chips, pine straw, and compost. A 1–2 in. layer of organic mulch on the soil's surface will serve also as a natural fertilizer as it decomposes. In addition, mulch also benefits the tree by helping to retain soil moisture, reduce weed growth, moderate extremes in soil temperatures, and protect the roots. Do not mulch a tree too heavily, and do not mound mulch against the tree's trunk. Both will cause serious damage to the tree over time.

Biostimulants are natural products containing beneficial bacteria and fungi that help create a healthy root system for your tree. Root health is very important because, for the tree to become well established and to flower effectively, it needs good absorption of water and vital nutrients and minerals from the soil. Biostimulants are applied onto, or injected into, the soil. Detailed information on biostimulants is available on the Internet. Before fertilizing your garden, you should research products carefully. Read and follow all product labels.

Watering

Proper watering is crucial for plants, whether they are trees, shrubs, or herbaceous plants. A regular watering regime is essential for the success of a new planting. Established plantings, although usually more drought tolerant and resilient than new plantings, also benefit greatly from a consistent, proper watering regime, especially during extended periods of drought. Trees that are improperly watered or subject to severe fluctuations in the amount of moisture in the soil will usually not perform particularly well.

Knowing how to apply the right amount of water to trees is essential and often challenging. In most cases, giving a tree either too much or not enough water will cause unwanted stress. Plant stress can compromise the tree's growth rate, flowering capability, and overall health. In addition, a stressed tree is usually more susceptible to pests and disease, and severe damage or death may occur.

The specific watering amount depends on soil type, water pressure, the size of the area to be irrigated, the tree species, etc. Heavy, clay loam soil tends to dry out slower than sandy soil. Also, certain plant species thrive in high-moisture conditions, whereas others prefer drier, well-drained conditions. As a general rule, in a climate where supplemental irrigation is required and in a period of drought, long, infrequent watering is preferred over short but frequent watering. For example, in the heat of the summer when plants are not receiving enough natural rainfall, watering a tree for two to four hours once or twice a week will provide a deep watering, which will encourage the establishment and maintenance of a healthy root system. In contrast, short, frequent watering, such as irrigating five times a week for half an hour each time, will only moisten the surface of the soil, creating a plant with a shallow, vulnerable root system. Very often short watering periods will waste valuable water because much of it may evaporate in the hot weather, instead of penetrating the surface of the soil. This subject is an important one, and you should consult with your local water authority on water restrictions for the specific community where you live.

Unlike established plants, a newly planted tree will require additional care for a few years after planting. A new tree should be watered consistently during the growing season for at least the first two or three years after planting to ensure that it is properly established. This supplemental watering will allow the tree to develop a well-formed root system. In most cases, after a couple of years the tree can then be incorporated into an ongoing garden irrigation schedule along with other established plantings.

Landscaping with Flowering Trees

4

Now that you know all about planting trees, the question you may ask now is, "Where?" Many excellent landscape design books can help you answer that question. The subject is very important, and it is difficult for me to give you in a few paragraphs all you need to consider when determining where to plant your trees. But while there is a lot to understand, it is not an insurmountable task and will provide you and your family an opportunity to express yourselves on the outside of the house, much as you have undoubtedly done with interior design. If doing it on your own is too intimidating, many landscape contractors will be happy to work with you to make your dream landscape come true.

It is crucial to understand a flowering tree's function in the garden. Trees and shrubs provide the "bones" of the landscape because their structural and textural qualities form the foundation of a well-designed garden. Where to utilize a tree as a specimen, in a grouping, or as an espalier is important to know.

Landscape design is essential to the success of flowering trees in the garden. A poorly sited tree can become more of a burden than an asset. One of the most common miscues of gardeners, for instance, is failing to supply a tree with enough space to grow. It is easy to underestimate the overall spread of the tree. Ultimate size, including height and spread, of flowering trees is provided for each species in this book. Be sure to carefully select the appropriate site for each tree you select for your garden. Trees that are misplaced may have to be pruned regularly to control their size, and they often become disfigured and unproductive over time.

A second siting miscue is simply planting trees with no real plan or purpose. Placing a few trees and shrubs randomly through the garden can create a confusing, distracting landscape of limited effectiveness. Proper landscape design techniques can create continuity and excitement in the home landscape. Coordinated use of flowers, foliage colors and textures, textured bark, fruit, and interesting growth forms can add great depth to any landscape design. Strategically site flowering trees to achieve a specific purpose.

The following potential uses of plants will guide you on some of the ways to maximize the function of your flowering trees.

An **accent planting** is an attractive-looking tree that will add interest to the garden. An accent plant can offer interesting bark, contrasting foliage, flowers, or fruit and brighten up the landscape. An example would be using

115

a tree with variegated foliage to liven up a shady area of the garden. *Cercis canadensis* 'Silver Cloud' has speckled, variegated foliage that will offer an accent of color in a partially shaded garden during summer.

An **allee**, although not always practical for a homeowner, can be a very effective way to use flowering trees in numbers. An allee is a rather formal technique of planting trees lining both sides of a path or drive. This effect can be quite handsome, as was mentioned under *Laburnum watereri*, goldenchain tree.

A **grouping** is a number of strategically placed trees (alike or different kinds) in a cluster that achieves a harmonious look and function. If room is limited and a large quantity of trees is not necessary, a smaller grouping will maintain harmony on a reduced scale. Groupings in odd numbers, such as three, five, or seven, can provide a less formal, natural look. Planting a grouping of three star magnolias that function as a single planting can be more effective than one solitary tree.

A **specimen plant** is an individual plant that is featured as a stand-alone plant in the landscape. Specimen trees are plants grown by themselves in a lawn or garden area for ornamental effect, rather than being massed with other trees, shrubs, or evergreens. A strategically placed tree is considered a focal point or even the main attraction in the garden. In a large garden, several specimens may be clumped together in a grouping to create a bolder impact. These trees are typically planted far enough apart that they are still separate and distinct but provide beauty collectively on a larger scale.

Vinnie's Top Fifteen Flowering Trees

Trying to choose my fifteen favorite flowering trees is quite a challenge. Most reasonable people would limit the list to ten, but my rather undisciplined affection for trees precludes me from doing so. As a passionate plantsman and tree lover, to me plants are like old friends that brighten our lives and feed our garden souls. Each genus, species, and variety has its own unique, beautiful qualities, making it difficult to choose merely a handful as favorites. However, here is my best attempt to offer a few of my favorite flowering trees. These trees were chosen because of their superior aesthetic value, cultural adaptability, and function in the landscape.

1. Japanese stewartia (*Stewartia pseudocamellia*)
2. Korean mountain ash (*Sorbus alnifolia*)
3. Flowering dogwood (*Cornus florida*)
4. Doublefile viburnum (*Viburnum plicatum* var. *tomentosum*)
5. Bottlebrush buckeye (*Aesculus parviflora*)
6. Shadblow serviceberry (*Amenlanchier canadensis*)
7. Hally Jolivette cherry (*Prunus* x 'Hally Jolivette')
8. Leonard Messel magnolia (*Magnolia* x 'Leonard Messel')
9. Dove tree (*Davidia involucrata*)
10. Flowering apricot (*Prunus mume*)
11. Red chestnut (*Aesculus* x *carnea*)

12. Sourwood (*Oxydendrum arboreum*)

13. Sugar Tyme crabapple (*Malus* x Sugar Tyme ['Sutgzam'])

14. Eastern redbud (*Cercis canadensis*)

15. Japanese clethra (*Clethra barbinervis*)

A Few Exceptional Public Gardens Worth Visiting

One of the best ways to learn about flowering trees is to visit your local public garden. Arboreta and public gardens provide picturesque displays of, and useful information on, many of the flowering trees discussed in this book. For the gardener who is in the market for a new flowering tree, doing research on his or her own garden, or just wanting to stroll around and appreciate the sheer beauty of trees, visiting the local public garden can prove very valuable and enjoyable. Here is a listing of a few exceptional public gardens worth visiting.

Atlanta Botanical Garden
1345 Piedmont Avenue NE
Atlanta, GA 30309
www.atlantabotanicalgarden.org/home.do

Bayard Cutting Arboretum
440 Montauk Highway
Great River, NY 11739
www.bayardcuttingarboretum.com

Biltmore Estate
1 Approach Road
Asheville, NC 28803
www.biltmore.com

Botanic Garden of Smith College
College Lane
Northampton, MA 01063
www.smith.edu/garden/home.html

Brooklyn Botanic Garden
1000 Washington Avenue
Brooklyn, NY 11225
http://bbg.org

Chicago Botanic Garden
1000 Lake Cook Road
Glencoe, IL 60022
www.chicagobotanic.org

Cornell Plantations
One Plantations Road
Ithaca, NY 14850
www.plantations.cornell.edu

Duke Farms
80 Route 206 South
Hillsborough, NJ 08844
www.dukefarms.org
www.njskylands.com/atdukgar.htm

Hofstra Arboretum
Hofstra University
Hempstead, NY 11549-1000
www.hofstra.edu/COM/Arbor/index_Arbor.cfm

Lewis Ginter Botanical Garden
1800 Lakeside Avenue
Richmond, VA 23228-4700
www.lewisginter.org

Longwood Gardens
1001 Longwood Road
Kennett Square, PA 19348
www.longwoodgardens.org

Missouri Botanic Garden
4344 Shaw Boulevard
St. Louis, MO 63110
www.mobot.org

Morton Arboretum
4100 Illinois Route 53
Lisle, IL 60532-1293
www.mortonarb.org

Mount Auburn Cemetery
580 Mount Auburn Street
Cambridge, MA 02138
www.mountauburn.org

New York Botanical Garden
Bronx River Parkway at Fordham Road
Bronx, NY 10458
http://nybg.org

Old Westbury Gardens
71 Old Westbury Road
P.O. Box 430
Old Westbury, NY 11568
www.oldwestburygardens.org

Phipps Conservatory and Botanical Gardens
One Shenley Park
Pittsburgh, PA 15213-3830
www.phipps.conservatory.org

Planting Fields Arboretum State Historic Park
1395 Planting Fields Road
Oyster Bay, NY 11771
www.plantingfields.org

Scott Arboretum of Swarthmore College
500 College Avenue
Swarthmore, PA 19081
www.scottarboretum.org

United States Botanical Garden
245 First Street, SW
Washington, DC 20024
www.usbg.gov

United States National Arboretum
3501 New York Avenue, NE
Washington, DC 20002-1958
www.usna.usda.gov

Winterthur Museum & Country Estate
Route 52 (Kennett Pike)
Winterthur, DE 19735
www.winterthur.org

Noteworthy Mail-Order Nurseries and Helpful Web sites

The Internet can be a very valuable resource when trying to locate flowering trees for your landscape. This is especially true of new, unusual, and even rare plant varieties that are difficult to find locally. Many mail-order nurseries and garden supply companies provide excellent, select horticultural materials and plants for the home gardener. The following is a listing of some exceptional mail-order nurseries and helpful Web sites.

Broken Arrow Nursery
13 Broken Arrow Road
Hamden, CT 06518
www.brokenarrownursery.com

Camellia Forest Nursery
9701 Carrie Road
Chapel Hill, NC 27516
www.camforest.com

Collector's Nursery
16804 NE 102nd Avenue
Battle Ground, WA 98604
www.collectorsnursery.com

Completely Clematis Nursery
217 Argilla Road
Ipswich, MA 01938-2617
www.clematisnursery.com

Cornell Cooperative Extension—Gardening
Cornell University
Ithaca, NY 14853
www.cce.cornell.edu/gardening

Fairweather Gardens
P.O. Box 330
Greenwich, NJ 08323
www.fairweathergardens.com

Forestfarm
990 Tetherow Road
Williams, OR 97544-9599
www.forestfarm.com

Gardener's Supply Company
128 Intervale Road
Burlington, VT 05401-2804
www.gardeners.com

Gossler Farms Nursery
1200 Weaver Road
Springfield, OR 97478
www.gosslerfarms.com

Greer Gardens
1280 Goodpasture Island Road
Eugene, OR 97401-1755
www.greergardens.com

Heronswood Nursery
300 Park Avenue
Warminster, PA 18974
www.heronswood.com

Klehm's Song Sparrow Farm and Nursery
13101 E. Rye Road
Avalon, WI 53505
www.songsparrow.com

Meadowbrook Nursery / We-Du Natives
2055 Polly Spout Road
Marion, NC 28752
www.we-du.com

Niche Gardens
1111 Dawson Road
Chapel Hill, NC 27516
www.nichegardens.com

Plant Delights Nursery
9241 Sauls Road
Raleigh, NC 27603
www.plantdelights.com

RareFindNursery.com
957 Patterson Road
Jackson, NJ 08527
www.rarefindnursery.com

**Rhododendron Species Foundation
and Botanical Garden**
2525 South 336th Street
Federal Way, WA 98003
Mailing address: P.O. Box 3798
Federal Way, WA 98063
www.rhodygarden.org

Roslyn Nursery
211 Burrs Lane
Dix Hills, NY 11746
www.roslynnursery.com

Siskyou Rare Plant Nursery
2115 Talent Avenue
Talent, OR 97540
www.srpn.net

Wayside Gardens
1 Garden Lane
Hodges, SC 29695
www.waysidegardens.com

White Flower Farm
P.O. Box 50
Route 63
Litchfield, CT 06759
www.whiteflowerfarm.com

Woodlanders, Inc.
1128 Colleton Avenue
Aiken, SC 29801
http://woodlanders.net

Glossary

Accent planting: An attractive-looking tree or grouping of trees that will add interest to the garden but not be the focal point. An accent plant can offer interesting bark, contrasting foliage, flowers, or fruit and brighten up the landscape.

Allee: A formal planting of trees or large shrubs that lines both sides of a pathway or drive. In most cases, the trees planted in an allee are all of the same species or cultivar, so the allee is uniform.

Bract: A modified leaf arising below a flower or inflorescence.

Calyx: A collective term for all of the sepals, or the outer most components of a flower, which are structural in function.

Compost: A rich organic material composed of humus and other organic material. It is used to improve soil conditions.

Compound leaf: A leaf divided into two or more parts that share a common stalk. Compound leaves can be pinnately compound; leaves have the leaflets arranged along the main leaf stalk. Palmately compound leaves have the leaflets radiating from the end of the petiole, like fingers of the palm of a hand.

Cultivated variety, also known as garden variety: A variation of a species that is produced through breeding or selection. A cultivated variety, also called a cultivar, is most often of garden origin and not found in nature.

Cyme: A flat-topped inflorescence

Deciduous: Shedding leaves at the end of the growing season and regaining them in spring the next growing season.

Dioecious: With male and female flowers confined to separate plants. Sumac is an example of a dioecious tree.

Espalier: To train the main branches of a woody plant flat against a wall, trellis, or fence, resulting in a plant growing practically in one plane. Also, a plant so trained.

Evergreen: Retain leaves year-round.

Fastigiate: Having an upright, columnar habit, branches erect and close together.

Fireblight: A bacterial disease that is especially prevalent in plants in the rose family such as *Prunus*, *Malus*, and *Pyrus*.

Flower cluster: A generic term for a grouping of individual flowers or multiple flowers on the same stalk. Panicles, spikes, and racemes are rather complex inflorescences that may also be referred to as a cluster.

Grouping: A number of strategically placed trees (alike or different kinds) in a cluster that achieves a harmonious look and function.

Humus: A naturally complex organic material made up of plant matter or animal manure.

Leaf margin: The edge of a leaf.

Lenticel: A small, irregular shaped corky gland on the bark of woody plants made of loosely packed cells. It is used for gas exchange but also has ornamental qualities.

Loam: Soil composed of even amounts of sand, silt, and clay, offering good drainage and an excellent growing environment for a wide variety of plants.

Mass planting: A planting that uses one type of tree in significant quantities will create harmony and maximize the effect these flowering plants can have in the landscape. Similar to a grouping, but larger.

Mulch: A layer of material, usually organic, applied to the soil surface to suppress weeds, retain soil moisture, moderate soil temperature, and add organic matter to the soil.

Panicle: An inflorescence having multiple stalked flowers.

Peduncle: The stalk of a flower cluster or single flower.

Petal: A petal is part of the inner floral parts of a flower or the corolla of a flower. The corolla is the name for all of the petals of a flower collectively and is typically showy.

Petiole: The stalk of a leaf.

Screening: Trees that function as a physical and visual barrier in the landscape.

Soil pH: The measure of soil alkalinity or acidity. Soil pH is measured on a scale from 1 to 14, with 1 being the most acidic and 14 being the most alkaline. A pH reading of 7.0 is considered neutral.

Specimen plant: An individual plant that is very noticeable and is featured as a stand-alone plant in the landscape. In a large garden, several specimens may be clumped together in a grouping to create a bolder impact.

Stamen: The stamen is the male organ of a flower. Each stamen generally has a stalk called the filament and an anther on top of the filament.

Sucker: A shoot arising from the roots of a tree.

Throat: Refers to the opening into the lower end of the corolla (flower petals).

Topsoil: The uppermost layer of soil containing organic matter and microorganisms; this is where most of the biological soil activity occurs. Plants generally concentrate their roots in this layer of soil.

Trifoliate: Refers to a leaf made up of three leaflets.

Variety: A naturally occurring subdivision of a species having distinct and sometimes inconspicuous differences and breeding true to those differences.

Variegation: Striping, edging, or other marking with a color different from the primary color. Variegated foliage can have creamy white, gold, or other showy colors contrasting with the basic green.

Watersprout: Fast-growing branch that grows straight up from horizontal branches.

Bibliography

In addition to the websites listed in the "Noteworthy Mail-Order Nurseries and Helpful Websites" section, many other websites and books were used in gathering the information found in *Great Flowering Landscape Trees*.

Bailey Hortorium. *Hortus Third.* New York: Macmillan, 1976.

Bartram's Garden. "The Franklinia Story." Philadelphia: Author. http://www.bartramsgarden.org/franklinia.

Berkeley Horticultural Nursery: Heidi. "Oh, Those Yellow Magnolias." Berkeley, Calif.: Berkeley Horticultural Nursery, 2005. http://www.berkeleyhort.com/gardensuggestions/gs_jf05_yelomagnolias.htm.

Brand, Mark. "UConn Plant Database of Trees, Shrubs and Vines." Storrs: University of Connecticut, 1997–2001. http://www.hort.uconn.edu/plants.

Burns, Marilyn K. "Magnificent Magnolias." Southern Great Lakes Gardener: Gardening Resource and Information. 2006. http://gardengal.net/page13.html.

Cornell Cooperative Extension of Nassau County. "Horticulture Fact Sheets." East Meadow, N.Y. http://www.ccenassau.org/hort/html/fact_sheets_home_hort.html.

Dirr, Michael A. *Dirr's Hardy Trees and Shrubs.* Portland, Ore.: Timber Press, 1997.

———. *Manual of Woody Landscape Plants: Their Identification, Ornamental Characteristics, Culture, Propagation and Uses*, 5th ed. Champaign, Ill.: Stipes, 1998.

Evans, Erv. "Plant Fact Sheets." Raleigh: North Carolina State University, College of Agriculture & Life Sciences, NC Cooperative Extension, Horticultural Science, 2000–2005. http://www.ces.ncsu.edu/depts/hort/consumer/factsheets.

Farlex, Inc. "Garden." The Free Dictionary. http://www.thefreedictionary.com/garden.

Fort Valley State University, College of Agriculture, Home Economics and Allied Programs. "Crape Myrtle—Pruning." Georgia Extension Teletips 716. Fort Valley, Ga.: http://www.ag.fvsu.edu/teletips/trees/716.cfm.

Gardiner, J. M. *Magnolias.* Chester, Conn.: Globe Pequot Press, 1989.

Hillier Nurseries. *The Hillier Manual of Trees and Shrubs*, 8th ed. Newton Abbot, England: David & Charles, 2002.

Kelly, John, ed. *The Hillier Gardener's Guide to Trees and Shrubs.* New York: Reader's Digest, 1997.

Knox, Gary W. *Magnolias.* University of Florida IFAS Extension, Environmental Horticulture Department, Circular 1089. Gainesville: University of Florida, Institute of Food and Agricultural Sciences, 1994. http://edis.ifas.ufl.edu/MG270.

PlantExplorers.com. "*Davidia involucrata*: The Dove Tree." http://www.plantexplorers.com/articles/davidia-involucrata.htm.

Rakow, Donald A., and Richard Weir III. *Pruning: An Illustrated Guide to Pruning Ornamental Trees and Shrubs.* Ithaca, N.Y.: Cornell Cooperative Extension, 2005. Downloadable through http://hdl.handle.net/1813/3573.

Rutgers, the State University of New Jersey, Office of Corporate Liaison and Technology Transfer. "Venus: Cornus × 'KN30-8'." Rutgers Ag Products. New Brunswick–Piscataway, N.J.: http://agproducts.rutgers.edu/venus.html.

Shaughnessy, Debbie, and Bob Polomski. "Crabapples." Clemson, S.C.: Clemson Extension, Home & Garden Information Center. http://hgic.clemson.edu/factsheets/HGIC1007.htm.

Weir, Richard, III, and George Good. *The Cornell Guide to Planting and Maintaining Trees and Shrubs.* Ithaca, N.Y.: Cornell Cooperative Extension, 2005. Downloadable through http://hdl.handle.net/1813/3572.

Whitinger, Dave. "Gardenology." Bryan–College Station, Tx.: Dave's Garden. http://davesgarden.com/terms.

Wikipedia, The Free Encyclopedia. http://www.wikipedia.org.

Index of Scientific Plant Names

Index of Common Plant Names

Index of Common Plant Names

About the Collaborators

Vincent A. Simeone

Vincent has worked in the horticultural field for over twenty years. He has degrees from Farmingdale State University, the University of Georgia, and the C. W. Post Campus of Long Island University. Vincent has specialized expertise in woody plant identification, plant culture, landscape use, and selection of superior varieties. Vincent is also an experienced lecturer, instructor, and horticultural consultant. He continues to promote innovative trends in gardening, such as proper plant selection, four-season gardening, integrated pest management, and low-maintenance gardening.

Vincent A. Simeone and Pickles

Vincent teaches a diverse assortment of gardening classes and has assisted in special garden tours to many beautiful gardens in southern England, northern France, southern Germany, Ireland, Canada, New Zealand, and South Africa. Vincent is also very active in the community on local, regional, and national levels with garden clubs, horticultural trade associations, and public garden organizations. Vincent currently works in public horticulture, managing Planting Fields Arboretum State Historic Park in Oyster Bay, New York.

Bruce Curtis

Bruce has chronicled many of the significant events of the last decades of the twentieth century as a photographer for *Time*,

Bruce Curtis

LIFE, and *Sports Illustrated.* He has been on the front lines of the Vietnam War, covered the explorations of Jacques Cousteau, captured the glory of the Papal Archives, and chronicled the action on the fast-paced sports field.

His uncanny ability to capture the significant moment led Bruce to explore special effects with MIT electrical engineering professor and strobe photography pioneer Dr. Harold Edgerton. Bruce's interest in action photography inspired him to use pyrotechnics and laser light to create the "action still life," a combination of the best of special effects and still life photography in one dynamic image. The demand for his images in posters, calendars, books, greeting cards, and CD-ROMs continues to grow. Bruce's studio is located on Long Island, New York.